"In *Joining Forces*, Jeanie Miley tackles one of the great themes of this and all eras—namely, gender identity, roles, conflicts—and brings clarity, reason and great feeling to bear. She ranges freely between the scholarly and the personal, and while examining the issues through a Christian lens, she embodies insights from depth psychology, which are provocative and enlarging. This book deserves to be read for it will leave the reader more thoughtful, and no doubt a freer, more emancipated person for having read it."

—*James Hollis, Ph.D., Jungian analyst and author*

"*Joining Forces* explores the primary Christian responsibility to love—both self and others—from the perspective of gender. It is the deeply moving story of one woman's coming of age in the 1960s, in a conservative Baptist tradition, believing Paul meant it when he said "In Christ there is no male or female." . . . She helps us to see one another with loving eyes, seeking the person in the image of God too often hidden by masks and stereotypes. "

—*Diana Garland, Ph.D., Dean, Baylor School of Social Work*

"Jeanie Miley writes from a deep well of concern about gender imbalance and a lifetime of perceptive observation of the damage it does to both women and men. Even if you do not share her Jungian perspective of the nature of the masculine and feminine dimensions of human life, you will find her insights about *Joining Forces* for the healing of the gender war inviting and constructive. She rightly understands its foul fruit to be a spiritual problem, and her significant experience in spiritual direction grants a distinctive wisdom. I have been moved by her stewardship of her life and training to write such a timely book."

—*Molly T. Marshall, Ph.D., President and Professor of Theology and Spiritual Formation, Central Baptist Theological Seminary*

"In this honest and very personal book, Jeanie Miley provides a creative and impassioned response to the "gender wars," calling men and women to recognize similarities and differences as signs of a common humanity. Blending her own experiences with other diverse voices, she offers spiritual guidance and pragmatic strategy toward a new paradigm of male/female relationships and honest communication."

—*Bill J. Leonard, Wake Forest University Divinity School*

Smyth & Helwys Publishing, Inc.
6316 Peake Road
Macon, Georgia 31210-3960
1-800-747-3016

Printed in the United States of America.

The paper used in this publication meets the minimum requirements of
American National Standard for Information Sciences—
Permanence of Paper for Printed Library Materials.
ANSI Z39.48–1984. (alk. paper)

Library of Congress Cataloging-in-Publication Data

Miley, Jeanie.
Joining forces : balancing masculine and feminine / by Jeanie Miley.
p. cm.
ISBN 978-1-57312-507-9 (alk. paper)
1. Man-woman relationships—Religious aspects—Christianity.
2. Sex role—Religious aspects—Christianity. I. Title.
BT705.8.M55 2008
248.8'4—dc22
2008013921

JOINING FORCES

Joining Forces

Balancing Masculine and Feminine

Jeanie Miley

Dedication

With love and gratitude

to Martus

and
to my daughters,
Michelle, Julie, and Amy

Acknowledgments

In reflecting on the countless women and men who have shared their stories and wisdom, hopes and dreams, failures and success with me over the years, I must say that I have been abundantly blessed with friends, soul friends, and teachers.

I am astounded as I recall the privilege I've had of learning from some of the best teachers imaginable. Their gifts to me are precious and sacred, and I hold them with a deep sense of awe, respect, and delight.

My interest in "balancing masculine and feminine" began when I was asked to lead a group of women in a self-discovery group in the early 80s. This book was born with the brave and loving women in San Angelo, Texas, who met for two years in three separate spiritual growth seminars I titled "Joining Forces," and then fleshed out in retreats, workshops, and seminars. It's been a long but loving labor.

I am indebted to the women in the Thursday Morning Bible Study at River Oaks Baptist Church, the men and women in my Sunday school class, and the Monday Night Bible Study at St. Luke's United Methodist Church in Houston. You have journeyed with courage and love with me, and I love you for who you are and for what you have called out in me. You have been my teachers. *Thank you.*

I am profoundly grateful for the friends and for my family who have encouraged and challenged me and for those who have agreed with me and for those who have not. I stand on the shoulders of magnificent human beings who have opened my mind, my heart and, sometimes, doors of opportunity for me.

I am so grateful to all of you.

Jeanie Miley
April 15, 2008

Also by Jeanie Miley

Becoming Fire

Christheart

Ancient Psalms for Contemporary Pilgrims

Sitting Strong: Wrestling with the Ornery God

The Spiritual Art of Creative Silence

Contents

Introduction

At some point, someone has to stand up and be the adult and start the forgiveness process.

—Mike Poe

"Love one another. . . ."

—John 13:34

I was born female.

As a young girl approaching womanhood, I could never have imagined the changing roles of women, the drastic societal changes in marriage and family life, or the ongoing and shifting aspects of what has been called the gender war. The movies and magazines of my adolescence didn't prepare me for the future.

I was born the much youngest third daughter, into the home of a Baptist minister. Born at the end of World War II, I am neither a war baby nor a boomer. I was born in Sweetwater, Texas, and except for the five years I lived in New Mexico, I have lived my entire life in Texas.

Those ordinary facts reveal the most significant forces that shaped the formative years of my life. My family of origin, the location and time of my birth, my position in the family, the lifework of my father, and the fact that I was born female were the forces in forming many of my beliefs about myself, the world and my place in it, and God.

I absorbed the rules for being female from my family and the culture in which I grew to adulthood. I formed beliefs about a man's role and a woman's role based on what I observed and experienced; mostly, those beliefs had to do with what men and women *did* (their roles) rather than who they *were* (their personhood).

Those unconscious beliefs and rules about men and women had to do with spirituality and sexuality, work and play, health and happiness, and the use of time and money. I came of age and entered adulthood with beliefs I had been taught; more important and powerful were the mindset, opinions, and feelings that I had caught from my environment.

At first, I didn't understand the gender war. As far as I was concerned, there wasn't one. Looking back, I realize that there was no war apparent to my young eyes because everyone behaved within their culturally defined, fixed roles, doing what they were supposed to do.

It worked . . . until it didn't, and it was the noisy revolutionaries who rattled the cages of the status quo, waking us all up to the factors that had numbed us into slumber in the first place, factors that needed to be named and confronted. Perhaps things hadn't worked as well as I'd thought.

There are those who have tried to ignore the gender war or control it through various means, some of them regressive and denigrating to both men and women, but the truth is that the culture of today is vastly different from our parents' and grandparents' culture. Yesterday's answers to issues of gender balance are no more adequate for the complexities of today's world than they are in the realms of science, medicine, and technology. The answers I carved out in my youth are not adequate for my daughters.

There is enough blame to go around when it comes to gender imbalance. Men and women have hurt each other in different ways through the generations. Part of the sense of being wounded in our culture originates in our belief systems about what it means to be male and what it means to be female.

While it is simple and popular to point to men and patriarchy as "the problem" in the gender war, there is another point of view that allows both women and men to be a part of the solution. At the root of our gender conflicts is an overvaluing of masculine strengths such as independence and competitiveness and the undervaluing of feminine strengths such as cooperation and adaptivity. In overemphasizing either feminine or masculine strengths, we draw on only half our strengths.

If we were to swing too far in the opposite direction and overvalue feminine strengths and undervalue masculine ones, and if we were to create a matriarchy, that too would be an imbalance, fueling another set of problems.

Within every human being, female or male, are both masculine and feminine characteristics. Obviously, we lead with our most natural strengths and characteristics, but we can learn to expand our options in relating to each other and in becoming more creative when we recognize, access, and express those strengths that are either unrecognized or undeveloped.

It is my belief that in accessing our feminine strengths, *the joining, connecting, and relating strengths*, we can move toward both an inner and outer balance, and by joining masculine and feminine forces, a person can relate in healthier ways to both men and women.

While I write from my own point of view, I have worked to understand the point of view of men. I've listened to men and women, and what concerns me is that all of us are wounded. I have listened to people from vastly different cultural groups, and I have listened to individuals from different generations. All that I have heard has increased my compassion for human beings as we are attempting to make a living, raise a family, pay the bills, balance the competing demands of daily life, and somehow stay healthy and safe. My compassion has increased for men and women, people attempting to live in a rapidly changing world in which what we learn in school is often outmoded by the time we enter the "real" world.

I write this book with the constant buzz of a rapidly changing, pluralistic culture in my head. I am frequently reminded that we all come from vastly different belief systems and cultural mores; I acknowledge that I speak from my personal worldview. Beneath all the things that make us different, I believe we will find basic human longings and similarities that will help us reach out in compassion and understanding, forming connections of acceptance and celebrating the fact that we are all members of the same family.

Both women and men, overusing our masculine strengths, are in danger of destroying ourselves with an incessant need for power and control. We are desperate as a culture for the forces that I call the *joining* forces. To correct our dangerous imbalances, we must grasp and then express the forces that connect, unite, and restore us, traits that men and women alike can and do express. We must become more open and generous with each other. Our "joining" strengths restore us to our own souls, our own creative energies, and our own true, essential natures.

All of us are struggling to do the best we *can* do, even as we do not seem to be able to do the best we *know.* I have come to believe that women do not win if men lose—and men do not win if women lose. No one of us really has authentic power if we are depriving another of power.

"Are you going to tell us what to *do* to end the gender war?" I've been asked this question repeatedly, and I always respond the same way.

In the first place, it isn't my style to tell others what to do, and besides, this isn't a "Ten Easy Steps to Ending the Gender War" manual. I can't offer a product at the end of each chapter, and I can't guarantee results. Human beings are not machines. We are complex creations made in the image of God. We cannot take our minds, our souls, or our relationships to a mechanic for repairs. There are solutions and methods that can help us win friends and influence people, facilitate communication, increase intimacy, and build community, but this book is an invitation to a process of soulwork. *Soulwork takes time.*

From the beginning chapter, then, this book is not a how-to manual, which is a masculine form, but an exploration, which is a feminine form. The "answers" and "what to do" are not in the chapters, but will be discovered as you join your life experience with the concepts and thoughts within the chapters. I have, however, included questions for reflection and suggestions for action at the end of each chapter.

I am fond of the image of life as a journey, and I have found that the inward journey is one of the most challenging and exhilarating journeys of all.

Joining forces, making connections, and loving each other along the way are all challenge and reward.

Made in the Image of God

"Look! I am making everything new!"

—Revelation 21:5

Human beings, we are told, carry within themselves a very great possibility and corresponding to this possibility, a great obligation. We have the possibility of opening ourselves to a quality of life and consciousness that transcends anything we ordinarily experience as happiness or knowledge or meaning.

—Jacob Needleman

I am always learning....

—Michelangelo

What is woman, that you rejoice in her,
And man, that you delight in him?
You have made us in your image,
You fill us with your Love;
You have made us co-creators of the earth!
guardians of the planet!

—Psalm 8:4-7, Nan Merrill

Some people believe that the gender war is over.

However, the current political climate and the accompanying profusion of opinions about gender and race convince me that there are still barriers to confront and bridges to build across the chasms between us.

When I consider the issues of human trafficking, gender injustice in Third World countries, the disproportionate weight of the AIDS epidemic on women and children in Africa, gender imbalance in the workplace, misogyny in the church and in society, and the various forms of religious, emotional, physical, and spiritual abuse and violence against women and children around the globe, I feel overwhelmed by the needs in the world. Sometimes I get so overwhelmed that I just want to pull the covers over my head and return to the warm womb of denial and unconsciousness.

When I hear men and women lament the difficulties of relating to each other and when I cringe at sexist jokes from either gender, I know that we are not where we need to be as human beings.

Our culture is too complex for simplistic solutions, and yesterday's answers are absolutely inadequate for today's challenges and problems. When I don't know what to do next, I *can* go to work on one thing at a time, and I can do the next thing indicated.

I am proposing that the next thing indicated for us as individuals is to make peace with the masculine and feminine parts of our inner lives. That peace just might make it possible for us to reach out more confidently and courageously and join forces with another man or woman, connecting at a soul level with honor, respect, empathy, and compassion.

Step by step. Day by day. Person by person.

There is no way to peace, the sages tell us. Peace *is* the way, and it begins with me.

"I want to be close to Beth, but I'm almost afraid of her," the young man told me. Karl was thirty, well-educated, handsome, and articulate. (While writing this book, I was granted permission to use some real full names; where confidentiality is required, I have used fictitious first names alone.) "About the time I think I can risk being close to her, she starts acting bossy and pushy, and I just go into my cave and stop talking to her. I really like her strength, but sometimes she goes too far or I get scared."

As I listened, I remembered the things Beth had told me about her father. I wanted to say, "If you knew her history, you'd understand why she does what she does," but it was up to Beth to disclose what she wanted Karl to know.

Later, Beth told me, "I'll never give up my freedom! I'm scared of being alone, but I'm more scared of being controlled and being hurt! I really love Karl, but he can't seem to accept me as I am. We're in a standoff; I can't end the relationship, but I don't feel safe in it."

Of course Karl had trouble with Beth! Until he faced his own issues with his "inner woman," he would be repeating his patterns of a lifetime over and over, contaminating the present with the past.

Two lonely people, each hiding in a cave of fear, each wanting to connect with the other but too scared to come out of their defended places. Both people are strong, and each is successful in the external world, but they are unable to trust or love each other.

"My friendship with Sue is over," a woman told me. "She is so competitive with me that I can't stand it. Why can't we accept each other and enjoy each other and not have to play those awful power games?"

"I'm a project to my mother," a twenties-something woman told me recently. "She doesn't understand why she can't get the same results from me that she gets from her charts and graphs at work. I'm a *person.* I'm not a *project,* and I won't be another award she can nail to her office wall!"

Joining forces with any other human being, connecting at a deep level, is an act of strength and faith. Often, people hide out in separateness, protecting their own independence in power struggles and power moves.

Men and women will always be different, and individuals are different from each other, but it is time for us to come out from our hiding places, our separate rallies for individual rights, and come together in helping each other become whole. Joining forces requires a healing and a reclaiming of our feminine strengths; when we do that, we become more balanced and effective, and we are more fully reflecting the full image of God instead of a half image.

Over the years, my interest in the intricacies and complexities of relationships and how our relationships reflect our various images of who God is has led me down many fascinating paths. Trying to unlock some of the mysteries of relationships, I happened upon an idea that made sense to me. I repeat it here because it is foundational: *Within each of us, men and women alike, we all have both feminine and masculine strengths and capacities, and each of us is more fully human when we can access the relevant strength in the appropriate measure for the current situation, whatever it may be.*

My daughter Julie proves the primary thesis of this book when she talks about the field of medical research, a field formerly considered a male-dominated field. In fact, men and women researchers use both masculine and feminine strengths, relying on hard data, charts and graphs, logical thinking and advanced training in highly specific and technical areas, *and* their intuitive thinking, open-mindedness, receptivity to new ideas, and sometimes, I'm confident, sheer gut instincts. Both men and women combine masculine and feminine strengths to explore far horizons and discover healing modalities and life-giving procedures.

Moving beyond constricting and limiting concepts—such as "women are emotional" and "men are competitive"—and accepting the fact that we *all* can be emotional help break open some of the boxes in which we've placed ourselves, freeing us to learn how to do what needs to be done in the moment. In the beauty of irony, I believe that males become more fully actualized and well rounded by accessing, integrating, and expressing their feminine side, and females become more fully actualized and well rounded by accessing, integrating, and expressing their masculine traits! We all move toward wholeness when we access, embrace, and accept all parts of our capacities.

When I expressed these concepts to Ben Thurman, a physician who is trained in both Western and alternative medicine, he jostled my thinking and stunned me with another dimension to the issues of the gender war, commenting on how the dress of women, particularly the huge shoulder pads of the power suits, was indicative of women's attempts to appear strong and powerful.

Dr. Thurman said, "When women overuse their masculine strengths, attempting to right the wrongs of the past, it is as if they become inferior males, and when men try to express their feminine sides at the expense of their masculine nature, it is as if they become inferior females."

Wow! Not only did this physician get it, but he articulated one part of the gender problem succinctly and clearly. What he said is only one part of the problem between the genders, but it is a big one. The old order is gone, but we're not quite sure about how to behave in this new order!

"You women act like men," a male character in *P.S. I Love You* (Warner Brothers, 2007) says to an aggressive female, "and then you don't like it when we don't want you."

Ugh. Another expression of the bigger problem.

A recent quote in an ad in *Vogue* magazine indicates that perhaps women have made a little progress in accepting ourselves as strong and powerful. "We don't have to dress like boys to be taken seriously," says Michelle Cooper, identified only as a plastic surgeon in the ad. "Most men expect us to look feminine. It's just important that when we speak, we are confident."

Perhaps power suits were and are necessary, but the shoulder pads can go. Women might have needed them in the '60s and '70s, but we've grown up since then. At Christmas, my three-year-old grandson opened one of his gifts, a football jersey and helmet, gleefully exclaiming, "Now I can play *baseball*!" Sometimes, you can have on the costume and not know what game you're playing!

I have no illusions that this book can end the gender war. Frankly, I am staggered by the enormity of the topic. I cannot attempt to solve all of the problems related to gender imbalance. However, I propose that we can move toward understanding, compassion, and loving-kindness for one another by doing these things:

1. We can wake up.

Anthony de Mello says that spirituality is about waking up, and waking up some more. "Most people," he says, "are born asleep, they live asleep, they marry in their sleep, they breed children in their sleep, they die in their sleep without ever waking up" (*Awareness: The Perils and Opportunities of Reality* [New York: Image, 1990], 5).

Each of us must wake up and become conscious of our own attitudes, our history and baggage, our own biases, prejudices, and blind spots, our behavior and the way it affects other people. Self-awareness is not self-absorption or narcissism; it is the necessary first step in any effective communication between human beings.

Who we are as men and women is a profound spiritual issue. Becoming whole, healthy, and more fully human is one of our tasks. It is a sacred responsibility.

2. We can respect each other as people.

Instead of seeing ourselves and each other through the lenses of rigid role definitions and our own notions of how a man should be or what a woman should do, or hemmed in by our gender role expectations or constraints, we must learn to see each other as individuals and as human beings *made in the very image of God.*

Becoming more awake and aware, we see each other as human beings instead of objects to fulfill our own needs or expectations. We respect one another as mysterious and unique. We do not lump people into groups, but allow individuals to be who they really are, starting with ourselves.

As I was completing this manuscript, I opened the February 18, 2008, issue of *Newsweek* to a book review of a new book, *What Shamu Taught Me about Life, Love, and Marriage* by Amy Sutherland, animal trainer and journalist who decided to apply the techniques of animal training to her husband. "Want an obedient spouse?" the headline asks, and then declares, "A new book says you should coach them like animals."

We have a long way to go.

3. We can get acquainted with the masculine and feminine strengths within every man and woman, and we can learn how to use each strength appropriately.

With knowledge comes a wider range of freedom, choice, and effectiveness. As self-knowledge and awareness increase, we can know when we are out of balance, overusing one strength until it becomes a weakness, and we can correct the imbalance by calling upon another strength. We can learn to become more proficient at moving back and forth between our masculine and feminine strengths, as a situation demands, becoming more balanced, more creative, and more productive in that dynamic process.

4. We can stop projecting and start relating clean and clear.

Without awareness and asleep at the wheels of our lives, we project what we don't know about ourselves onto other people. We see others not as they are, but as we are, and so sometimes see anger in someone who isn't angry. We attribute motivations to others that are actually lurking in our own unconsciousness, and sometimes we fall in love with another's gifts or greatness rather than owning and taking responsibility for our own. That is why Jesus said we are judged by the way we judge others (Matt 7:1-2)!

We also seem to project our unconscious feminine and masculine traits onto others. Carl Jung theorized that a man projects his feminine self onto a woman and a woman projects her masculine self onto a man, and in doing so, it is as if they become blind to who the person really is. In the grips of a projection, we are not in the present moment and the person in front of us is not who they really are. Instead, voices from the past and unconscious entanglements with people in the past cloud our vision and prevent us from relating to the person in front of us.

"Every time I talk with that person, I feel as if I'm talking to my *mother,*" a woman told me one day. "Is that about you or is it about her?" I asked, and we laughed.

"I feel like I'm five years old when Arthur's around," a man told me. "He's not my father, but when I'm with him, I can't stop thinking about my father!"

To establish and maintain real relationships, we have to stop projecting our own inner pictures onto another innocent human being, asking him to "carry" our self-made masculine or feminine images. We can stop projecting our own needs onto others, allowing others to be who they are without asking them to be "mother," "father," or countless variations of those roles for us.

For more than twenty years, the issues that affect men and women have fascinated me, but never more than today as I observe the struggle for gender equity and peace in the outer world and as I enjoy my own daughters with their children, boys and girls, in this brand new world of possibility and change.

Using my feminine strengths of receptivity and openness, I could listen and research for this book forever. That feels natural to me because I love the asking, seeking, knocking, and exploring of research.

To move into my masculine strengths and become decisive—closing the door to further research—is painful for me. I resist having to set time and space boundaries and meet deadlines, but if this project is going to be a book, I must utilize both my feminine and masculine strengths to their maximum potential. In a sense, the partners within each of us must learn how to dance better together.

"What do you mean by this masculine self and feminine self?" Thomas, a workshop participant and longtime marriage therapist, asked me when my husband and I were leading a workshop for the Texas Association of Couples for Marriage Enrichment. We had just presented a brief overview of the concept of "joining forces."

"Sounds a little Jung-y to me," said another, and his colleague quickly responded by reminding him that Jung is not on trial. Admittedly, some would argue with that.

As I began explaining the idea that each of us has masculine and feminine traits, Thomas interrupted me. "Are you talking about *androgyny*?" he asked, and I could feel myself getting anxious and fearful of his rejection. "Do you want us all to be alike?" he continued, and I could feel his scorn.

"I'm talking about becoming more balanced and whole and expressing the full range of characteristics that God packed in you when he made you and then using those skills to become more creative and productive and more connected with the people who matter to you!"

At the end of our presentation, a respected marriage therapist and friend said to me, "This makes so much sense, and it is such a simple, yet profound, part of all our relationships. It helps me understand my frustration, too, in that I've spent so much time trying to become sensitive and tender that I sometimes feel I've lost my masculine strengths!"

"I hear you," his wife told me later, privately, "but I'm afraid to reclaim my feminine strengths. I'm afraid that if I'm too adaptive or too cooperative, I'll be run over at home and at work! I've worked hard to gain the power I do have; I don't want to go back to the old ways."

As I understand the biblical revelation, God has been inviting us into relationship—a covenant relationship—from the beginning. Our joining strengths will reconcile us to God, just as the life and teachings of Jesus liberated people from the chains of religious legalism.

Joining strengths put us in harmony with nature, our own bodies, and those around us. Indeed, joining or being open to joining requires vulnerability, courage, accountability, and honesty, but the payoff is that we can heal our inner fragmentation and outer separation and unite with each other in new and healthier ways. Instead of being in competition with each other, we can join the dance of reciprocity, mutuality, giving and receiving and help each other become whole.

As vulnerable as it makes us, joining, connecting, relating, and cooperating are imperative strengths if we are to succeed.

As scary as it is, it is time for us to *love one another.*

"Come now, let us reason together," God said to the children of Israel through the prophet Isaiah (Isa 1:18).

"Be kind and compassionate to one another, forgiving each other, just as in Christ God forgave you," Paul counseled the women and men at Ephesus (Eph 4:32).

We can and we must learn how to use masculine strengths, our reason and logic, and our feminine strengths of kindness and compassion as we learn to love one another into fullness, wholeness, and health.

Here and there, men and women are growing beyond the need to demand their rights, recognizing that if someone has to lose in order for someone to win, then no one has really won. Like a delicate crocus pushing up through the snow of winter, there are signs of hope pushing up through our hardened, old patterns. In some places, people really are living out the freedom of Christ in relationships.

The good news about men and women may not make the headlines, and it isn't yet drawing a crowd, but men and women are learning to come together in new and improved dynamics, relating to each other with the appropriate degrees of respect, equality, and assertiveness. In places, persons are intentional about becoming more fully human, accessing both masculine and feminine strengths, for the good of all.

In 1991, I gathered with a group of people at Laity Lodge for a Writers' Retreat with Madeleine L'Engle, my dear friend and mentor. I could hardly wait for this retreat, for each retreat had been so productive and helpful. Being with Madeleine was like being with an Earth Mother. Madeleine was deeply attuned to nature and to others, and many of us felt the warmth of her nurturing presence. I know sometimes that must have felt like a burden to her, but she was always welcoming and generous.

A couple of years before this retreat on a hot summer afternoon at Laity Lodge, I'd sat in her room while she patiently dictated her "alphabet of prayer" to me, a prayer she recited as she walked from her apartment in New York City to the library of the Cathedral of St. John the Divine. Later, she cooked lunch for me, a peanut butter and bacon sandwich, in the kitchen of the retreat center. Madeleine was strong and tender, powerful and wise, and being with her was life-affirming and life-giving.

As we gathered for that retreat, we were tense and anxious, for it was also the beginning of the Gulf War. Like a good parent and responsible retreat leader and citizen, Madeleine arranged for us to receive reports of the war twice a day, but in the meantime, she said, we were supposed to go about our business. At every session, Madeleine L'Engle spoke of the urgency of the need for love and kindness. Often, Madeleine said, "Every act of kindness ripples out and out and out, like a pebble thrown into a pond, and you have no way of knowing what that ripple will touch."

Treating one another as human beings made in the image of God—starting with our own lives—is radical kindness.

This book is a pebble thrown in the pond; may its ripples bring wholeness and reconciliation, person by person.

Questions for Reflection and Discussion

1. Where do you see gender imbalance in your everyday life?

2. How are things different between men and women today from the expectations you had growing up? What has been gained? What has been lost?

3. What do you think needs to happen to facilitate gender peace?

4. What has been the biggest surprise to you about men in the last decade? What about women?

5. If you could make one change in yourself in relating to men, what would it be? What about in relating to women?

6. What kinds of wisdom would you like to pass on to the next generation to make things more harmonious between men and women?

7. What do you consider the basic needs of each gender?

Taking Action

1. The next time you are talking to someone else, listen for any gender issues that might come up in the conversation, either in jokes, slurs, put-downs, or insults. How do you feel when you hear/say those things?

2. For a day, be intentional about giving respect to a person of the opposite gender. Pay attention to the response to that respect.

3. Watch the dynamics between persons during the day. Note instances when you see obvious respect from one person to the other.

Start with Yourself

Everyone, man or woman, contains possibilities for both masculine and feminine development, and no one can approach wholeness without some development in both areas."

—John Sanford, *The Kingdom Within*

Justice itself is rooted in the reality of the incarnation, for when God made mankind, he made us male and female—in his image. To do injustice to anybody is to do injustice to the reality of God, because we are in his image, and his image is not to be demeaned. —William Shaw

"The Kingdom of God is within you."

—Luke 17:21

"Who are you?" the man asked me.

I told him my name, and he asked me again, "Who are you?"

I told him that I was the wife of . . . , daughter of . . . , mother of . . . , graduate of . . . , and he was still not satisfied.

"Who are you without those other people?" he demanded.

It was my first small group experience, and I was in for the ride of a lifetime.

How would you answer that question? Would you identify yourself by the roles you play? the degrees you hold? your professional title?

We present our verbal resumes to each other all the time, getting acquainted and establishing our credibility by what we tell others about ourselves.

"Who are you behind your persona?" the man continued, probing, and finally I said, "*I am a woman!*"

"You are?" he asked. "What does that mean? What kind of woman are you?"

Frustrated, I stuttered out some adjectives. Married. American. Young.

Some might identify themselves by family, a cultural or religious identity, or by character defect as in "I'm an addict" or "I am a codependent." For some, being identified by their wounds is the entry point into making connections. For others, "I'm a survivor" is an important assertion, an affirmation of having overcome something that was potentially life-threatening.

"Are you who others have told you that you are," the man asked, "or are you who you know yourself to be?"

Whatever the roles we may play in life, it is the *person,* made in the image of God, who is unique, unrepeated in humankind, and of infinite value. That original essence is the person we are created to be, the authentic self, who we are at our core. Some say that it is the soul. Still others call that essential self the *imago dei,* the image of God.

A primary aspect of that identity is that within each of us are what have been characterized as masculine and feminine characteristics. An important task, then, of maturing for men and women alike is to learn how to use our various strengths—masculine and feminine—in the appropriate way, at the appropriate time, and in the appropriate measure. In doing so, we have the opportunity and obligation to seek the balance of those energies and strengths. As the masculine and feminine energies within each person learn to work together, we are better at joining forces with men and women in the outer world.

It sounds easy, doesn't it?

So what's the problem?

It seems that it should be simple to access and express both feminine and masculine energies and attributes, but for a long time and in ways that have been practiced so long that they seem normal, the feminine energies have been denigrated and devalued and the masculine energies have been elevated and seen as superior.

When a person is cut off from his or her feminine energies—which happens to men *and* women—there will be an imbalance within that individual. It follows then that an internal imbalance will be expressed outwardly in relationships with others.

In his essay, "The Recalibration of Gender Relations," in the book *Finding Balance: Reconciling the Masculine/Feminine in Contemporary Art and Culture*, Leonard Shlain asks us to imagine a stroke victim who is paralyzed on one side of his body. In that tragic condition, that human being is trying to function with only half his capacities or less ([Houston: Houston Center for Contemporary Craft, 2007], 21).

Shlain, surgeon and world-renowned author and lecturer, says, "The image of a hemiplegic is an apt metaphor for the present state of gender relations in many parts of the world. Observing the daily news, evidence abounds that many societies repress women, thoroughly suffocating their creative potential" (21).

It seems logical to me that when feminine traits are devalued, dismissed, and demeaned, it follows that women will also be devalued. When feminine strengths are repressed, women will be repressed, no matter what the outer rules, laws, policies, and rhetoric may be.

It is possible for women to break through glass ceilings. By law or under pressure, a woman can hold positions of power, prestige, and privilege, but there can still be disrespect *for* her and *from* her if there is an inner imbalance in her and in the people with whom she works.

Later in the essay, Shlain says, "The happiest and most successful contemporary societies are those in which women have achieved near equal parity with men in terms of political, economic, and social power. The general quotient of productivity, abundance, democracy, and tolerance is the highest in those places where men and women behave with respect and compassion toward each other" (21).

My belief is that the happiest and most successful people are those who are able to access and express both masculine and feminine strengths. I believe we move more surely toward productivity and abundance on the outside when there is more democracy and tolerance on the inside. Balancing masculine and feminine strengths is a way of living more nearly as a person made in the image of God. Respect and compassion are crucial in joining together and working for good, and those qualities cannot be faked.

What does it mean that each man and each woman has both masculine and feminine strengths? My friends in recovery programs counsel me to "keep it simple" when things are most complicated. How, in this new world of confusion about gender roles, can simplicity lead us out of the gridlock and into more smoothly flowing traffic patterns of relating to each other?

Perhaps nature can help us. Nature seems to carry and operate with the play of opposites: Hot/cold. Wet/dry. Night/day. Up/down. Active/passive. Static/dynamic. Right-brain/left-brain.

Masculine/Feminine.

And the truth is that every one of those qualities exists on a continuum, doesn't it? Every one of us has each of those capacities and qualities, but in different degrees. Maybe we could be more creative if we could begin to think of these traits as existing and moving on a continuum instead of in polarities.

In his book, *Masculine and Feminine: The Natural Flow of Opposites in the Psyche*, Gareth Hill uses the infinity symbol, a universal symbol, to communicate the importance of the flow of energies within a human being ([Boston MA: Shambhala Publications, 1992], 24, 26, 36). Hill further separates the various qualities into dynamic and static feminine qualities and dynamic and static masculine ones, an idea that expands the concept of feminine/masculine strengths. Hill's suggestion that immaturity keeps us stuck in only one aspect available to us also invites us into the possibilities of learning, changing, and adapting to become more whole and healthy.

Throughout history, that which is called "the feminine" has often been symbolized by a circle or a chalice, and "the masculine" has been represented by an arrow or a blade. Feminine strengths have been about receiving, connecting, and holding, while masculine strengths have been about separating, making decisions, taking action.

Working with these ideas, I have compiled a list of masculine and feminine strengths, gathered from a host of writers, teachers, and thinkers, and it is always interesting to me to observe reactions to the lists. As you read over them, suspend judgment and simply open your mind to the idea that all the strengths are valuable and that the capacity for all the strengths, to one degree or another, exists in every human being.

Masculine Strengths

strong
concrete
relational
logical
individualistic
independent
decisive
closed
pronouncing
religious
controlling
risk-taking
factual
methodical
analytical
forceful
action-oriented
left-brain
bold
territorial
self-contained
result-oriented
firm
confident
powerful
leading
precise
objective
straight-forward
focused

Every person needs to be able to express masculine strengths. These strengths are necessary when we need to make decisions, classify information, segment and differentiate one thing from another. Masculine strengths help us take action and organize data, people, and ideas so that they are useful. Our masculine strengths are helpful in developing self-reliance and in setting appropriate boundaries.

Without masculine strengths, any person can become weak, powerless, and soft. An overuse of masculine strengths, on the other hand, can cause individuals to be authoritarian, bullying, or rigid.

Feminine Strengths

warm
compliant
conciliatory
open
receptive
flexible
adaptive
listening
nurturing
cooperative
intuitive
right-brain
abstract
emotional
spiritual
responsive
sharing
trusting
process-oriented
giving
sensitive
consulting
accommodating
dependent
vulnerable
containing
embracing
diffused
thinking
exploring
subjective

Every person needs feminine strengths in order to grow, because it is the feminine strengths that are open to new possibilities and processes. Feminine strengths help us in the give and take of everyday life. They help us in building consensus and forming teams. Appropriate dependence allows a person to yield to another's expertise or leadership, rely on another person, and trust someone else.

Without appropriate feminine strengths, a person can become close-minded and stubborn, self-centered and detached from feelings and instinctual energies, and insensitive to others' needs. An overuse of feminine strengths can lead to moodiness, neurotic caretaking, and hypersensitivity.

Whenever a group reflects on these lists, regardless of the venue or the ages of the participants, a discussion of the interplay of feminine and masculine qualities is guaranteed to set off an animated response.

A consistent response of women who look at this list of feminine qualities is to express a feeling of shame about their feminine strengths. Generally, a woman in the group will say, "When I exhibit any of these qualities, I feel weak," and someone else will say, "I feel vulnerable; using these qualities makes me open to being hurt." Now and then a woman expresses satisfaction or pride in the expression of her feminine strengths.

At the same time, women often shudder when they read the list of masculine strengths, often responding with, "I don't like this about myself," or "This is what my (mother)(husband)(friend) doesn't like about me." There are *names* for women who overuse their masculine strengths!

Women often talk about how they are expected to use masculine strengths in the workplace and lament that those same strengths, used at home, don't have such good results. In a mixed group, men will often remain silent while women take over the discussion until I call attention to the silence of the men and invite them into the dialogue. Repeatedly, the group is stunned to hear what men have to say when they are given a chance to speak in an environment that values both men and women and recognizes that both masculine and feminine strengths exist in all persons.

Invariably, someone takes the conversation to the issue of extremes, reminding all of us that any strength carried too far becomes a weakness. Any one of these strengths can become an instrument in the abuse of power, either by a man or a woman. We are all out of balance on any given day, and we unconsciously overuse what is natural, comfortable, and familiar to us. Some of us don't even know that we have certain strengths because we've been so programmed by our culture in role rigidity.

Always, the conversations raise other questions. Does biology determine destiny? Why is it so hard for us to talk about what it means to be a "real" woman or a "real" man?

In this era when all the rules and roles are changing, how can the simplicity of a concept about masculine/feminine energies help us resolve some of the gridlock in relationships between men and women? We won't know until we try, will we?

The truth is that women and men alike have been hurt and have hurt others when expressing their feminine strengths, and we are all afraid of being vulnerable, open, and transparent. We have all been hurt and have hurt others when misusing our masculine strengths.

As mature and responsible adults, we can admit that our culture overvalues masculine strengths and undervalues feminine strengths in either men or women and that we have problems related to that state of affairs. We aren't bad people because we have problems; instead, the problems can provide us the opportunities to learn and change, grow and expand our minds, hearts, and souls.

My daughters are all in their early thirties, and each of them brings information and perspective from a different professional world. Each sees through the lenses of her own temperament and life experiences. Though they grew up in the same household with the same parents, each has a distinctive point of view about what it is like to be a woman in today's culture.

Sometimes an awareness of the difference between my experience of growing up female and my daughters' experience growing up female is almost breathtaking to me. When they ask me questions about my experience as a young girl or woman, the look on their faces fascinates me, for I can see that much of what formed me as a woman is all but incongruous to them.

I need to listen to them about their world regularly so that I will not forget how varied and wide are the human experiences and so that I will avoid getting stuck in my own point of view, thinking it is *the* prevailing one! I want to know about the shifts and changes in interpersonal relationships my daughters are experiencing, and I enjoy watching their children, boys and girls, grow up in a world my parents could not have imagined. Much of what separates us about gender issues in families, churches, groups, and nations is a matter of generational differences.

"I want to hand down what I know to my children," mothers sometimes say, forgetting that what we long to hand down often is irrelevant, outmoded, and unwanted!

Underneath the generational divides, however, flow streams of commonality that we share because we are human beings, first of all. With my daughters, there is a connectedness that goes back to my mother and her mother and forward into their children, a connection that has been most profound as my daughters have given birth to their own children.

About once a year, I would like to do the children's sermon, the same sermon, at my church. I imagine how the children would look—girls and boys together—at the front near the altar, wiggling and squirming with promise and potential . . . and a fair amount of impatience and restlessness.

First, I'd ask the children to sing "This Little Light of Mine" with me. I'd want them to hold up their index fingers just as I did in children's choir when I was a child. I hope they wouldn't be as shy as I was about performing in public.

In my sermon I would talk to the children about the Light of Christ and the light of their own uniqueness. I would want them to know that they are made in the image of God and that when their light shines, everyone benefits.

I would make a big point about how Jesus' message is to all of us, female and male, telling us that we must let our lights shine. As I read it, Jesus didn't have any exclusions in his injunction!

Together, we would sing, "Hide it under a bushel—No!" Each of us would cup one hand over the "light," and then remove that covering quickly when we shouted, "No!" Then I'd want us to talk about what it means to hide your own light.

People do hide their own lights from each other, and we are infinitely creative in the ways in which we do that. We may run from responsibility and run from growing up. Sometimes, we are afraid of rejection or ridicule, and at other times we are afraid of success. We may hide the light that is in us because we're afraid of showing off or because someone has told us that only certain people are allowed to shine. Even grown-ups, now and then, are afraid of breaking the rules or the status quo, and that may be important for children to know! The bottom line is that hiding our lights is all about fear.

It's a big responsibility, after all, to let your light shine, and shining takes courage and persistence. You have to keep your wick trimmed and oil in your lamp, to use biblical images, and you may need someone in your life who is willing to say to you, "Take the bushel basket off your light and *let it shine*!"

After we sing the verse about "not letting Satan blow it out," I might have to do a little teaching about who the devil is and who he isn't, as I understand that, of course, and I know I'd have to say that it is a dangerous thing to mess with the light of someone else and to prevent another's light from shining.

I want the children in my church to know that what you do to another, you're really doing to yourself. When you blow out the light of another person through discouragement, criticism, or acts of exclusion, and when you prohibit, either by neglect, ignorance, or outright willfulness, the expression of giftedness in the life of another, you are snuffing out your own light. When you diminish another, you diminish yourself, and when you do it under the banner of the Bible, there's something insidious and evil about it.

Well-meaning people do the most damage in extinguishing the light of others, using Bible verses to justify an allegiance to role constraints, rules, prejudices, and biases. People blow out others' lights by a habitual and unconscious loyalty to the status quo, by ignorance, and by fear. Power struggles, jealousies, and outright meanness cause people to snuff out the light of others who might threaten their positions or privileges.

It's a risky thing to put yourself out there and let your light shine, being fully who you are. Letting your light shine leaves you open to others' criticism. Not letting it shine is a sure road to depression, despair, and sometimes death.

I have been fascinated by Jesus' allowing his inner circle, Peter, James, and John, to see the full blaze of who he was in that moment on the Mount of Transfiguration (Matt 17:1-13). Even Jesus took a risk, in a way. His friends, disciples-in-training, could have said, "Hey, who does he think he is?" or "Whoa! You're coming on a little strong there." Ultimately discerning, Jesus knew how to manage the Light within him. He knew when and where and how and in what measure to manifest the fullness of himself, and he knew the people who could handle his Light.

Singing that last verse about letting our lights shine "till Jesus comes" would give me an opportunity to talk about how long it takes for some good things to happen. I would talk about the necessity of patience, persistence, and the willingness to keep on keeping on, and by then, the children in front of me would be ready to go to Children's Church. I might entice them to stay a little longer if I asked them to turn around and lead the congregation of adults in singing the song with them.

I'm betting that some of those adults may have forgotten about letting their lights shine. Some may not have known they had a light at all.

Perhaps all of us, men and women alike, could use a little experience in reminding each other of the Light that is within us.

Questions for Reflection and Discussion

1. As you read the list of masculine traits, what did you think? What did you feel? Did you argue with the list?

2. As you read the list of feminine traits, did you have a different kind of reaction from the reaction you had to the list of masculine traits? What did you think? What did you feel?

3. In what settings do you feel most comfortable expressing feminine traits? In what settings do you feel most comfortable expressing masculine traits?

4. In what settings do you feel that you allow the light that is your uniqueness to shine, unhindered by fear on the inside or others' responses from without? What is that like for you?

5. How do you hide your own light?

6. Have you ever participated in snuffing out the light of someone else?

Taking Action

1. As you go through your day, look for people who are letting their lights shine. Describe that person.

2. Ask someone to give you feedback on how they perceive you in relation to the two lists of characteristics.

3. Listen for others' statements of self-deprecation. Keep a list for a week and see who does it more, men or women.

Harnessing the Energies of Love

Someday, after we have mastered the winds, the waves, the tides and gravity, we shall harness for God the energies of love. Then for the second time in the history of the world, we will have discovered fire.

—Teilhard de Chardin

Consider well the essence of love,
the echoes of mercy and justice . . . . Psalm 48:13, Merrill

The subject of men and women, of the nature of the masculine and the feminine, always arouses our interest, especially now, when men and women are trying, as never before, to understand themselves, and when the roles of the sexes and their relationship to each other are being reexamined. It is also a practical subject, promising to give us useful information that we can apply directly to ourselves and to our personal relationships.

—John A. Sanford

I imagine it is a crisp winter day when two hundred men and women, clergy and lay leaders in various denominations, gather at a conference center near Atlanta, Georgia, to spend three days exploring ways to bridge the gender gap.

In my dream about such a meeting, over dinner the first night, and before the opening session, there is an air of controlled excitement and a seeming heightened respect for each other. The participants are serious about their assignment.

At the opening session, the convener explains the format. He says that in all of our discussions, we must keep the following ideas in mind. In fact, these statements are written and displayed in each meeting room at the conference center:

- We need to learn how to say hard things without creating barriers between us.
- We need to learn how to hear hard things without becoming defensive.
- We need to be *intentional* in communication that will build bridges between us.

Quietly and with a high level of energy, participants move from the large group to smaller meeting rooms in groups of twenty. Seated in concentric circles with chairs facing each other, ten women and ten men of diverse cultural, ethnic, and racial groups, single and married, divorced and never married, and ranging in ages from twenty-nine to seventy are led through various exercises designed to facilitate understanding, empathy, and compassion for the opposite gender.

As I've envisioned this meeting, a group leader, trained in group dynamics and communication skills, guides the process in each room, making sure it is carried out in an environment that provided safety for each participant. Safety is easy; comfort isn't quite so easy as men and women look each other in the eye, speak hard things with honesty, vulnerability, sensitivity, and transparency, and hear hard things with openness, receptivity, and a surprising lack of defensiveness.

At the beginning, the questions would be designed for low-risk self-disclosure.

- Where did you grow up?
- In what ways did the place where you grew up shape your view of yourself as a man or a woman?
- When did you first realize there was a gender gap?
- Do you think the gender war is over?

As the process continues, the questions would become more challenging.

- What were "the rules" about "being a man" and "being a woman" in your hometown?
- What happened to people who didn't keep those rules?
- What kind of prejudice against the opposite sex did you witness when you were growing up?
- What did your church teach about women's roles and men's roles?

By the last day, and before the wrap-up sessions in the large group, the questions would move into some more sensitive areas.

- What did your father teach you about being a man, both verbally and nonverbally?
- What did your mother teach you about being a woman?
- Were you welcomed as the gender you are, or did your parents want a child of the opposite gender?
- What is it like for you now, as a man (or a woman)?
- What would you like to tell the people closest to you about who you are?
- What do you fear most, as a woman (or a man)?
- What prejudices and biases do you have about the opposite sex?
- What would you like to see repaired for future generations?
- What would "gender peace" look like?

Such a meeting exists only in my imagination and in my hopes and dreams. The idea for it was born, however, as I flew home from Atlanta to Houston last January after having attended a meeting with twenty other women, laity and clergy, at the headquarters of the national office of the Cooperative Baptist Fellowship in Atlanta. At that meeting, we explored the changing roles of women within our denomination and the various ways we could support women in our churches. As we talked, we acknowledged a desire to work better with each other, male and female.

When my husband had taken me to the airport to fly to Atlanta, the last thing he'd said to me about the meeting was, "Don't leave us out, Jeanie. Don't leave us out."

His words haunted me all through the meeting, and I knew that I had to speak them at some point. It's common for women to get polarized in "womanthink," forgetting that when any homogeneous group gets together, it's easy to get stuck in the same place, saying the same things and bending under the weight of a one-sided point of view.

It has never been my intention—ever—to leave out men, except of course when they want to be left out! I happen to like men, in general, and I love the men who are in my life. I stand on the shoulders of men who have befriended and encouraged me, opened literal and figurative doors for me, provided for me, and helped me do things I could never have done on my own.

Most of the men in my life have been honorable men who have been fair and played fair. Most of the men in my life want equality for their wives and daughters, friends and colleagues, and many of them have worked to provide opportunities for women in leadership roles, sometimes stepping aside to allow a woman to have a chance to advance her own goals.

Some of the men in my life have grown weary of the enormous effort it takes to make sure everyone has a chance, and some report to me that after gargantuan efforts to put women in positions of leadership, they have endured the wrath of other women who felt they had been excluded! Other men tell horror stories of watching women hurt each other in terrible ways. Some of my friends who actively support women in leadership speak about not wanting to be the brunt of the wrath that belongs to others, *both male and female,* who denigrate women in any way.

However, I am keenly and personally aware of the ways in which women are still bound by prejudices and biases. I am aware of the abuse of women in both subtle ways, and in outrageous, visible acts of violence. I know that patriarchal systems still do their work to keep us in rigid patterns that inhibit creativity, foster perversions and mistrust, and perpetuate hatred and fear.

As I have written this book and listened to current political and cultural conversations, I am appalled at what is clearly disdain for women, and underneath that, a denigration of "the feminine." I am appalled at the ways in which women hurt each other, often through gossip, innuendo, passive aggression, covert sabotage, and knives to the back. I am deeply saddened by the ways in which women project their own self-hatred onto specific women. Indeed, I have come to believe that women have unconsciously absorbed misogyny, the hatred of women. News articles reveal that catfights common to women are being seen in young girls' bullying of each other.

On the way home from Atlanta, I did get lost in a fantasy about what might happen if there could be a meeting such as the one I described in the opening of this chapter. Since that wasn't immediately possible, I decided to do the next thing indicated and submit my ideas to my publisher, ideas I have addressed for more than twenty years in retreats and workshops.

I came of age in the mid-sixties, part of the generation born right before the Baby Boomers, but not really part of the World War II generation. I was in what was probably the last group of women who, for the most part, planned on being wives and mothers with credentials in either teacher or nursing "for insurance."

For most of my life, I scheduled my writing, speaking, volunteer work, and teaching around my family's needs. Hearth and home were my first priorities, and I feel a deep sense of gratitude and contentment that I was able to do what I did with those years of my life.

My consciousness began to change as I started designing and leading weekly spiritual growth groups for women and conducting retreats and workshops for both men and women. Over and over, I heard successful women, both homemakers and those in the workforce, express increasing fears about being vulnerable, open, and receptive, even with each other, or, sadly, *especially* with each other. I listened to couples grappling with the impact of their changing roles.

In spiritual growth groups, I listened as women talked about how they had become so competitive, independent, and task-oriented that they were feeling awkward just being friends with other women. Some spoke with disdain about trying to converse with stay-at-home women, but they also spoke of missing the mutual nurturing and nourishing of female friendships. Stay-at-home moms, working women indeed, expressed their feelings of being devalued and belittled, often by a look or by silence in conversations with career women.

I hear women express a soul suffering and a frustration at not being able to fulfill the call of God within their own communities of faith, and I have struggled mightily with that in my own life. Men, searching for ways to relate to "the new woman," have become more tender and sensitive, only to discover that there are still distances between themselves and women. Men and women in marriage enrichment retreats increasingly expressed frustration at trying to reconcile what they had been taught in church and what they had learned about being a man and being a woman in an era of transition and chaos.

Aaron Kipnis and Elizabeth Herron list these and other different points of view that exist between men and women in their book *Gender War, Gender Peace* ([New York: William Morrow & Co., 1994], 21–22).

- Men fear women's power to wound them emotionally, and women fear men's power to wound them physically.
- Women feel sexually harassed; men feel sexually manipulated.
- Men say that women are too emotional; women say that men don't feel enough.
- Men are often afraid to speak about their own vulnerability and victimization; women frequently deny their real power and capacity for abuse.
- Women feel that men don't listen; men feel that women talk too much.
- Many men believe that they must become more like women to be whole; and many women are trying to be more like men.

Kipnis and Herron add that "Both women and men have lost connection with a powerful, sacred image of masculinity and femininity that is a balance with the other sex," and it is that reconnection, the joining of the masculine and feminine forces within each human being, that this book addresses.

When I began working with the ideas in this book in the early 1980s, the women's movement was becoming unpopular, but it was then that I began hearing in both men and women a longing for reconciliation. Women had broken through the glass ceilings in various areas, and, in some places, the role of women in the church was beginning to change. As always, though, the church has been the caboose on the train, following far behind the culture.

In many places, the reaction to the women's movement was beginning, though it took time for me to realize the impact or scope of the reaction. I could never have imagined that there would be women who would want to disregard the strides that had been made in bringing some degree of equality into the workforce, especially from women who were the beneficiaries of their militant predecessors!

A woman in her early forties told me recently, "I realize that I am able to do what I do because my mother did what she did, and I don't need to forget that."

Looking back on the decade of the 1990s, I am fascinated by the fact that it became politically incorrect even to talk about the women's movement. Women kept entering the workforce, advancing in education and in their careers; however, they were also doing "the second shifts" at home. In the meantime, society hit the rapid waters of change in every area. Fundamentalism, and with it a hierarchical model of marriage and family, grew, and yet, *something* was happening within individual men and women, in relationships, and beneath the surface of family life.

I see women who are trying to overcome the oppression and misogyny of history and who are working so hard to push down their feminine strengths that they lose some of their greatest power! I see women attempting to overcome oppression, both real and perceived, and straining to gain a place for themselves and bring balance in a world of inequities. In doing so, they overuse masculine traits, become abrasive, and often lose the very things for which they've worked. How sad it is to watch women manifest the same traits they have found so offensive in men!

I see men, attempting to cooperate and collaborate with women, becoming passive out of fear of over-expressing their masculine power. Perhaps they are afraid of the anger of women, as well. I see men becoming comfortable with their nurturing and tender sides, only to be told by their wives that they aren't doing *enough.*

The pain and frustration that I hear from both men and women is far more than confusion about the division of labor within the home or the mistreatment of one sex by another. It's not about who takes out the trash or who earns more money, though our inner wars often get played out on those fields.

The pain I hear cannot be solved by enacting another law, changing the language in hymnals, or declaring a "year of the woman." Somehow, something internal in individuals must shift in order to move women and men into a new day. Knowing oneself, talking and listening, laying down defensiveness, and intentionally opening one's mind and heart all lay the groundwork for understanding each other, healing our broken hearts and relationships, and restoring society. It's an enormous challenge, and the truth is that the more potential there is for intimacy, the more potential there is for pain.

My dinner partner asked me what my writing project was about and then listened politely while I explained the thesis of this book. I could tell that she was waiting for me to cut to the chase and tell her how to repair her relationships in seven days.

"What can I *do*?" I, too, have often asked when faced with a situation I could not fix. I'm sympathetic with seekers who want a quick fix, an easy answer, a user's manual, or a Band-aid for a problem. If I can *do* something, I don't feel so helpless.

"*Be*, Jeanie. Learn to *be*," I've been told, and that response both irritates me and soothes me.

Anthony de Mello, Jesuit priest and writer, says in his book *Awareness: The Perils and Opportunities of Reality* that most people don't want to be cured. What most of us want is relief; to be cured is painful and takes longer.

"Awareness, awareness, awareness is the answer," I'm told. "Wake up. Pay attention. Be conscious. Change your mind. *Let it be.*"

I'm a daughter of my culture, an American raised on the work ethic, confident that if I work harder, longer, or smarter, surely I can fix whatever is broken or make faster or more efficient whatever I've got. I've lived my entire life in a religious culture that often seems to be more about American capitalism than it does New Testament gospel—bigger is better and faster is even better! Working at recovery from an addiction, working on relationships, and working to grow spiritually are important, and soul-work is hard work.

The life of the soul and the care of the heart are mysterious, watched over and tended by the One who is Mystery. The journey of the soul is a partnership, a collaboration—a dance, in fact—with life. It is a relationship with the One who created us, involving our connection to our innermost essence and with the individual people in our lives. I've often quoted the truth that "every meeting of persons is an exchange of gifts." The exchange between the various inner voices that people the kingdom within is also an exchange of gifts, and to know that and live that is the challenge of this book.

When it comes to the dynamics between a man and a woman, there are many things that could be interpreted as being "broken," and there is plenty of blame to pass around. It is in our female/male relationships where we often feel most vulnerable, most afraid, and most defensive, and when we are afraid, we often shut down, strike out, or head out to the farther plains of isolation. Often, we take on those relationships as projects that can be tweaked, trying first this theory or that in an attempt to adjust, change, or repair something sacred like a *relationship* with a bag of tricks or the latest tools.

I prefer to reframe the complexities of human relationship so that the places of pain and brokenness, conflict and misunderstanding are seen as invitations to wake up, grow up, and move toward wholeness, health, holiness . . . salvation. Indeed, dealing with gender issues must be approached with great tenderness and gentle firmness.

Most of us arrive at adulthood with archaic and unconscious programs about who we are and how we perceive ourselves as male or as female. Our programming shapes how we feel about ourselves and each other; informs our choices; dictates our perceptions, prejudices, and biases; and affects our behaviors.

Travis Perry, my longtime West Texas friend who's made a career of studying human behavior, told me recently, "Jeanie, those earliest tapes—those are the ones that are the hardest to erase." Indeed they are.

Jungian analyst and author (and former director of the Jung Center in Houston), Dr. James Hollis says that without consciousness, we live out our lives in an unconscious *repetition* of the patterns we learned in our families of origin. Sometimes we spend our lives *rebelling* against those patterns and sometimes we spend decades trying to *repair* those attitudes, habits, and behaviors we learned from our parents and are passing on to the next generation.

Awareness has the potential to bring about a change in the way you see yourself and others, and when you begin to change your mind, you can change your behavior. My own experience validates the theory that with increased consciousness and with a persistent and steady commitment to the challenge to wake up, changes begin to unfold naturally from within, and then, those changes are lived outwardly. The process can be slow and arduous, but over time, the experience can lead to healing, transformation, liberation, and empowerment.

I write not only as a woman, but as a person who has followed the path of contemplative prayer all of my adult life. The practice of contemplative prayer and meditation has shaped the way I approach the issue of gender balance.

What has happened in my external, everyday world has provided "seeds of contemplation" (to use Thomas Merton's phrase) for my meditation and prayer. It has been the inner connection with God-who-dwells-within that has pushed and sometimes shoved me into a new relationship with my outer world.

In her book, *Radical Wisdom*, Beverly Lanzetta says, "In Christian thought, the good 'active' life refers to all that we do to facilitate the journey—verbal prayer, good works, spiritual study and practice of virtues. The 'passive' reflects how the divine works in us, leading us through silence, receptivity, and openness to share in the intimacy of the divine life" ([Minneapolis: Fortress Press, 2005], ix).

My invitation is to join forces with the Divine Therapist, allowing the One who designed us to guide us to the kingdom within, where the masculine and feminine forces are recognized and made conscious. As that happens, we stop some of our self-defeating ways of working against ourselves and are able to join masculine and feminine forces together for our own good. That inner dance will then affect our outer relationships for health and wholeness.

"People are joining ballroom dancing classes by the hundreds," the commentator announced on a television news program, citing statistics at the beginning of a segment on the current wave that transcends generational boundaries.

For weeks, my husband and I joined several other couples in ballroom dancing lessons at a local dance school. "I can tell about a relationship between a man and a woman by watching the way they dance together," the instructor told us at our first lesson. That he might be able to see things we couldn't see about ourselves made all of us a little nervous, but the more we learned about dancing, the more we learned about ourselves.

"People danced separately in the seventies and eighties," he told us. "For whatever reason, men and women are suddenly wanting to learn how to dance together again, and so we are overrun with requests for classes."

Later, he said, "The challenge for both men and women is to learn to dance together again. It's as if we're having to learn how to trust each other and work together all over again." Indeed, we are also being invited to learn to know ourselves and each other, and that knowing requires openness, sensitivity, vulnerability, and courage.

"If you don't lead," our teacher often told the men, "she can't follow."

"Wait. Wait," he would tell the women. "Let him lead."

"This is a dance, not a competition," he sometimes said to the men. "If you make her look good, you'll look good, too!"

"Relax! Trust! Don't be afraid," he said to the women, and he had to say it often.

A lifetime of "dancing separately," going it alone, striving for *independence* calls for one set of skills. Learning to dance together, literally and figuratively, calls for another.

Questions for Reflection and Discussion

1. What person has been your most significant role model? What did you learn from that person?

2. What person has caused you the greatest amount of pain and suffering in your life? What have you learned from that person?

3. As you read about the fantasy meeting at the first of this chapter, what was your response? How would you feel about participating in such a conversation/meeting?

4. What do you fear most in relationship with women? with men?

5. As you read the list of different points of view from the book by Kipnis and Herron, which citation resonates most with you?

Taking Action

1. Invite another person to dialogue with you about the concepts in the first three chapters of this book. Set a time and space that is appropriate for a serious discussion. Practice listening carefully to each other; attempt to hear each other without passing judgment.

2. Peruse a variety of magazines. Ask these questions about the advertisements: Does this advertisement present a realistic picture of human beings? Is this advertisement demeaning of this person in any way? What is the hidden message in this advertisement, if any?

3. Make a decision about one relationship you would like to improve. How are you going to do that? What are the risks? What is the pay-off? Don't announce what you are doing; just do it.

Joining the Forces Within

"May they be one . . . as we are one . . . ."

—John 17:11

In the rocky shoals of life, much can be accomplished when we do not travel alone.

—Beverly J. Lanzetta

By healing the divisions in [ourselves we] would help [heal] the divisions of the whole world.

—Thomas Merton

And this is my prayer: that your love may abound more and more in knowledge and depth of insight . . . .

—Philippians 1:9

"I started to come to your workshop," an acquaintance said, speaking over his shoulder as we crossed a busy street outside the conference center in Washington, D.C., where I'd led a workshop on "Joining Forces." "I really was going to come, but I've already found my feminine side."

The man's buddies laughed, uncomfortably, and I played the good sport. I was pretty confident that he would rather have had a root canal than attend my workshop, but for some reason, he had taken note of the workshop in the program guide. I can't pretend to know what he was thinking, but I do know that many of us make jokes when we feel uncomfortable. Sometimes, when we are afraid, we assuage our fears by being cavalier or by diminishing or demeaning that which we fear.

It *is* hard to know what "this masculine/feminine stuff" really is and why it matters, and sometimes we're even afraid to ask. Athletes' weeping on the sidelines because they've lost a game may or may not indicate a connection with the feminine side, and a woman's wearing camouflage clothing could be interpreted a dozen different ways.

Robert Johnson writes of the importance of a man's "finding his feminine side" in his book, *He*, now a classic in male psychology. He writes, "Man has only two alternatives for relationship to his inner woman: either he rejects her and she turns against him in the form of bad moods, and undermining seductions, or he accepts her and finds within a companion who walks through life with him, giving him warmth and strength." Johnson goes on to stress the importance of the direct length, *the joining,* of a man with his inner feminine capacity for growth and creativity ([New York: Harper & Row, 1989], 34).

"If only we could all just go back to the times when it was easier," lamented a friend. "It was so much easier when our roles were clearly defined; everyone knew what to do then, and everyone knew their proper place."

She may be right, but there's no way we can go back in time—and I'm not sure it was all that easy "back then," whenever "then" may be. Indeed, when I look back on any time in my life, it does seem easier and simpler in some ways because I know more now. Life is on-the-job training for everyone. We sometimes romanticize the past to avoid the challenges of the moment.

Reflecting on my journey and the process of learning to balance my own masculine and feminine strengths, I recognize that the practice of meditation had a big part in waking me up to the need for balance. From my first contemplative retreat until now, the practices of meditation, silence and solitude, and centering prayer have been a vital part of my journey.

At my first contemplative retreat at the Church of the Savior in Maryland, I had the sense that a Power greater than myself had brought me to that retreat, that moment, that experience. The entire experience had a feeling of rightness and timeliness that gave me an internal sense of security. Looking back, I see now that that unseen Force was what we who call ourselves Christians call "Christ in me" or "the indwelling Christ."

What is called "practicing the presence of Christ" in everyday life turned my world upside down, frankly. Whenever I facilitate a centering prayer workshop, I tell the participants that I should put a warning sign on the door. In centering prayer, the process of prayer developed and taught by Thomas Keating, Benedictine monk and writer and founder of Contemplative Outreach, one's practice is a "Yes" to the *presence* and *action* of God in the interior depths of one's life, beyond the ego's domain and the conscious mind's control. That, of course, is what scares people!

When you show up for the discipline of meditation or centering prayer, you are giving assent to God to do what God chooses to do. This practice frees God, whom Keating calls "the Divine Therapist," to work in the depths of the unconscious, *changing the emotional programming of a lifetime* (for more on this, see Keating's book *Manifesting God* [Herndon VA: Lantern Books, 2005]).

The whole world of contemplative prayer, of which centering prayer is one aspect, is about giving up control, detaching from the need for results, listening, and being open, receptive, and vulnerable. It is the opposite kind of prayer in which the pray-er makes lists, informs God, and tells God what to do!

When I began the three-year program of training to become a spiritual director, Sister Mary Dennison wisely began the first retreat by explaining that it is the Holy Spirit who directs us, and it is our job to watch and wait, to look and listen, to discern the movement of the Spirit and move with it. Contemplative prayer is an agreement to move with the Spirit of God, the God who dwells within the human heart.

For me, this transforming, liberating, and empowering process has had much to do with bringing together my masculine and feminine energies. The Divine Therapist within has worked in this process to heal the parts of me that were wounded, change my thinking about myself as a woman, and empower me to live a more balanced life. In a sense, that inner process is about a profound change in the way my masculine and feminine strengths relate to each other in my inner landscape.

The process has not been linear, with a starting point and a logical progression of learning. Instead, it has been a circuitous journey. I have gone back to the same issues over and over in the process, but never precisely as I was before. I have regressed, sometimes in service to progress, and I have come to accept that this journey is a lifetime assignment. In many ways, I don't know what has been happening internally until I surprise myself with a change in behavior or attitude.

James Hollis speaks of the self not as a noun but a verb. He asks us to imagine that the Self is "selving." In other words, that life force within us is active and dynamic, moving us from within to be and do what we are created and intended to be and do.

What I did not fully understand at the time of that initial contemplative retreat was that the True Self/the indwelling Christ/God within was attempting to lead me *from within* to a deeper relationship with God by *compensating* for the action-oriented, results-focused religious world of my childhood and youth. God-within-me was leading me in ways I did not even know to an encounter with the part of God that I would find by abiding in him. God was trying to help me find more balance through the hunger for something more, the dissatisfaction with a law- and works-oriented spirituality. The One who had made me the way I am was leading me on a journey that would change my life through waiting, through listening for God, and in assuming a receptive and open heart and mind. Instead of a religious life that was all about reward and punishment, achieving and attaining, I was being drawn toward the contemplative world.

Early in my adult life, Andrew Murray's classic book on John 15 and the allegory of the vine and the branches, *Abide in Christ*, had fallen off the bookshelf and into my hands in the middle of a restless night (Greensboro NC: Christian Literature Crusade, 1972). I had been asking, seeking, and knocking to discover what it meant to "practice the presence of Christ." I was, indeed, weary and heavy-laden from trying to measure up to impossible standards of the work ethic of Christianity, and the way of "resting in God" was like balm to my soul.

Today, with the perspective of experience, I see now that God was attempting to heal my own inner separation between my masculine and feminine sides. In the way that God does, I was also being led *from within* out of a one-sided religious life that focuses on what is external and into what I've learned was a compensatory journey that would give me more balance. I was being led to the kingdom within.

Before I even knew very much about the theory of masculine/feminine energies within every individual, I would say, "Practicing contemplative prayer is like falling into the heart of God," and once I unconsciously spoke of contemplative prayer as being in the "womb" of God. Not even realizing it, I was using a feminine term, an intimate, relational term that would make some people nervous. In contemplative prayer, however, I was being asked to listen and receive instead of tell God what to do and how to run the world.

Through the years, I have repeatedly turned to Psalm 131 and imagined God stilling and quieting me like a mother quiets and soothes a child. I needed to let go of my taskmaster image of God and learn to rest in the arms of the gentle Mother, and that process continues. I have not arrived; I am still learning, and sometimes when I get too tired or stressed, I unconsciously regress to the old patterns. The difference is that I catch the regression sooner now and know what to do to return to balance.

As an English major, I learned to be comfortable with the pronoun "him"; as a woman I've tried to use gender-inclusive language, but, frankly, repetition of "he/she," "him/her," and "his/her" gets awkward. I don't image God as a glorified human being, but sometimes it is hard to talk about the Almighty without personifying him. (Nor do I know how to get around the pronoun problem when it comes to God or with humans!) With those disclaimers, I'd like to emphasize that when I use the masculine pronouns in this book, it is not because I see God as a man, but because I find that language fails me! I have no problem with the feminine side of God; what I stumble over is the bulkiness of language when I must use both pronouns to make sure I don't leave one out.

With that said, I must go on to say that I try to imagine the delight and joy of God when he pronounced his creation, woman and man, *good.* I can also imagine that God looks on those capacities and capabilities in each person, created in his very image, and is delighted when we use those gifts for good. My deep belief and conviction is that God does not assign a value—up or down—to either set of qualities and does not value one of them more than the others.

Human beings, on the other hand, have a little more trouble with each other and with the various strengths and weaknesses we bring to any encounter. We exist in a culture that influences us constantly, both directly and indirectly. Sometimes we don't even know how we feel and think about our own femininity or masculinity until we are confronted with new information, changing mores, or threats to our own sense of who we are in the world. I'm fairly confident that while most people have not reflected on their innate masculine and feminine strengths, every person thinks about how he or she feels as a man or a woman in relationship to others.

It seems to me that it is important that we hold God's view of who we are. It seems that it might be smart to value men and women in the way God does, and that constant change is part of the process and problem of being human. We are either growing or we are dying, and it seems to me that issues related to gender cause us to continue to grow and change.

Robert Bly, in the classic *Iron John: A Book about Men*, suggests that it is a good thing that men have developed their feminine sides, but he says that there is something deeper, perhaps a "Deep Masculine," which is vastly different from the savage man, that men must embrace and express. Clearly, men must keep growing and evolving, and the masculine within each of us can also keep growing.

Women, as well, need to learn how to use their masculine strengths better in order to become more balanced and to give support to their feminine strengths, but we do not need to give up our feminine strengths! Perhaps in the depths of who we are as women is a "Deep Feminine." The feminine within each of us can keep growing up, just as women must keep growing, developing, and evolving toward wholeness.

When I have presented the ideas in this book to groups of women and to mixed groups through the years, the responses to the material have changed. In some groups today, there is more lively discussion than when I first began talking about gender peace; in other groups, there is a silence that screams fear and resistance. Both the silence and the lively response are indicative of what was said by Laura Folse, speaker, community leader, engineer, and former Technology Vice President for British Petroleum's Exploration and Production Segment.

Speaking at a seminar on gender issues at St. Luke's United Methodist Church, Ms. Folse spoke from a practical viewpoint, emphasizing the facts about how *the gender war has gone underground*, and noting that when a person or a culture pushes something vital and important down into the unconscious or the unacknowledged, it doesn't go away. That which is repressed, suppressed, or oppressed will ferment until it finds a way to erupt into consciousness.

And so it seems to me that the Spirit of God may be at work in the area of gender balance, directing us to beam our attention, time, and affection toward efforts of reconciliation and restoration. Perhaps the Spirit of liberation is directing us to look at the ways in which we have bound each other in death wrappings. As we look at the problems related to gender, the wrongs inflicted on each other, and the abuses of patriarchy, perhaps we can see the agenda for the future. God is, after all, right in the middle of all things, attempting to bring about good.

We must keep opening up to each other and to new ways of understanding ourselves and others. We must keep on learning how to move, flex, and bend with the cultural changes. We must remain malleable so that we can respond to the promptings of the One who dwells and works within us and also dwells and works without us, among us, between us, and through us, attempting to bring about wholeness and harmony for us. It is hard for us to take a look at ourselves, especially in a culture that values action over reflection, and yet it seems to be true that what happens on the outside is the reflection of what goes on inside a human being. It seems true, as well, that what and how we think affects how we behave.

Doesn't it make sense, then, that knowing oneself is a good place to start in solving our personal problems? And since gender is such a vital part of our lives, doesn't it make sense to get better acquainted with both sides of our personality, the masculine and the feminine?

Indeed, our culture tends more to looking outside ourselves for the cause, blaming someone else for the problem, and trying to make others change and conform to the ways we think they should behave. We would much rather honk the horns of blame in the crowded intersections of our lives than own our part of the gridlock. It's more fun to pick at the specks in another's eye than to deal with the enormous planks in our own!

In his lectures, Dr. James Hollis fervently calls for a healthy self-reflection. He says that analysis and self-knowledge are not narcissistic or selfish, but are in fact acts of kindness and unselfishness to our families, our friends and coworkers, and ultimately to the larger world in that when we are conscious of our inner dynamics, we don't project what is inside us onto another innocent person, asking them to carry our projections. When we are conscious of our own motivations, thoughts, and feelings, we don't have to act out or take out our pain and problems, trouble and trauma on others.

Dr. Hollis often talks about starting with the symptom, that difficulty or painful outer world happening, the physical ailment, the depression or a relationship conflict, and tracking it back and back and back to its beginning point. Depth analysis is a process of "stirring things up from below" in order to bring that which is in the darkness into the light. So, it makes sense to take a look at those symptoms and see if perhaps there is a feminine or masculine strength that is being overused or neglected. Sometimes, we find our way out of the darkness by looking at our flaws or at our strength-pushed-too-far.

Any of the strengths or capacities, pushed too far, can become problematic for us, either interpersonally or within our inner lives. The corrective is often in becoming conscious, choosing an opposite strength, and acting to bring balance. To reflect the image of God fully, we need to know when to use which strength, and in the appropriate measure, at the right time and in the right way.

Perfection for me, at least on this side of eternity, is impossible, but the pursuit of wholeness and health is a journey I can take. Learning to access, embrace, and express both the masculine and feminine sides of myself is part of the journey of wholeness, a journey that fascinates and thrills me. It's a liberating and empowering journey, but like all spiritual quests, it is sometimes hard, laborious, scary, and painful.

At this point of my journey, I know that it's been worth the trouble.

Questions for Reflection and Discussion

1. List the reasons you think people are uncomfortable with a discussion about gender issues.

2. In what ways were things "easier" between men and women in the past? What do you think has been lost? What has been gained? Are the gains worth the cost?

3. Who do you think has benefited most from the changes in our society, men or women? Who do you think has been harmed the most? Explain.

4. Robert Bly indicates that men and women need to keep growing and keep becoming more of who they are. Where do you see men stuck in the feminine mode? Where do you see women stuck in the masculine mode? Where are you stuck?

5. Why not just "leave well enough alone" when it comes to gender issues? How can we know when things are well enough?

Taking Action

1. Watch a movie, noticing the dynamics between men and women. Do you like what you see? What makes you uncomfortable? What do you see that reveals something you want? Talk it over with someone.

2. Listen to music you enjoy and some you don't. What messages about female/male relationships are conveyed in the lyrics?

3. Express your feelings about something important to someone you trust. Risk a little and express your feelings about something to someone with whom you have a casual relationship. Which is scarier?

It's Not Your Mother's World (or Your Father's, Either)

There is ample reason for addressing ourselves to the question of relationships between male and female, and how we should live together as the image of God.

—Anne Atkins

So God created man in his own image, in the image of God he created him; male and female he created them.

—Genesis 1:27

There is neither Jew nor Greek, slave nor free, male nor female, for you are all one in Christ Jesus.

—Galatians 3:28

The development of both the feminine and masculine potentials in a person is also important for wholeness.

—John A. Sanford

"Angels rush in where fools fear to tread." In the opening lecture in his class "The Psychology of Love," Pittman McGehee began by turning a familiar quote around.

I actually thought he said, "Fools rush in where angels fear to tread," because that's how I'd always heard Alexander Pope's famous line (from "An Essay on Criticism"). It's funny how brains long accustomed to hearing things one way often miss fresh or innovative twists on deep truths. And sometimes it's not funny; sometimes it takes your breath way to realize how suffocating the belief system on which you've built your life, made your choices, and raised your family really are.

Indeed, the messengers who know anything about love had *better* rush in and begin talking and teaching about love, demonstrating love, and challenging others to choose love because the advocates of fear and the carriers of hate are working overtime to polarize us, make us afraid of each other, and drive us to hate each other.

What if men and women could learn to love each other as creations in the image of God, with mature and responsible love?

What if men and women could stop projecting their own unconscious issues about gender and their own need for a mother or a father onto others and started seeing people as individuals? *What if* we matured in our relationships so that when we say, "I love you," we didn't really mean, "I need you."

What if deep respect for "the other" was at the basis of our everyday encounters at the gas station or the deli, the boardroom or the bedroom?

On a beautiful spring day last year, I stepped up to the counter at a deli I frequent and asked about the decorated cookies. At that deli, named Picnic, Joe Bentley makes *the best* decorated cookies I have ever tasted, and I wanted to make sure I had plenty for my family's gathering over the weekend.

"He didn't make any today," the girl behind the counter said, but with the noisy din of the noontime crowd, I wasn't sure I'd heard her correctly.

"Did you say he didn't make any *today*?" I asked, hoping there would be some the next day.

"Yes, she said *he,"* the man in line beside me snapped. "Do you have a problem with a *man* baking cookies?"

Stunned, I looked up at him, and, confused, it took me a minute to get his point. He thought I was questioning the gender appropriateness, and I was merely asking about whether I could get cookies the next day!

The Picnic is a few short blocks from the Texas Medical Center and the Museum District, and within walking distance of Rice University. The man who snapped at me was well dressed, and later I noticed that he left in a fancy car. He was with a stylishly dressed woman, and as she walked away, she shot me an understanding look behind his back. I do think she had the grace to be embarrassed, but I'm not sure.

If I had had my wits about me, I would have made a comment about how most of the world's great chefs were men, but perhaps it was a good thing that I kept my mouth shut.

My daughter Julie was with me, taking a lunch break from her pediatric practice, and she made what my dad called "a few choice comments" under her breath. During her years in medical school and residency, she and I had talked about how different it was for her generation of women in the medical world than it was for earlier generations. Women who had gone before her had to use force and be tough in order to break through the barriers of a male-dominated world, and she knows that she and her peers are the beneficiaries of those bold women. Over lunch, we marveled about how even now, men and women still carry defensiveness and rancor toward each other.

While laws can and do arbitrate gender equity, the resentments and fears between men and women come out in quirky ways, at best, but often in violent ways as men and women continue to irritate and injure each other. Who would have imagined a gender conflict at the cookie counter in the heart of a neighborhood known for its polite society?

Only a few months later, a husband walked up to his dental student wife and shot her in front of her shocked fellow students and friends. He picked up her body and stuffed it in his car, drove to a church within a few blocks of my house, parked his car, and entered the church, announcing to persons in the church that he had killed his wife and that they needed to call the police. He walked back out to the parking lot and shot and killed himself. Newspaper reports made the point that he was failing in his career while she was soaring in hers.

The remark at the deli counter could just as easily have been made by a woman, and my city is famous for murders of men committed by women. Disrespect, disdain, sexism, racism, prejudice, and violence are not confined to either gender.

What's to become of us, male and female, created in the very image of God, and yet struggling in this new millennium to relate to each other in a world in which all the institutions we have known and looked to for stability and security are in flux? And how did we get to the place of making each other the enemy?

On a balmy Sunday afternoon a few days after my Picnic moment, I sat with a group of two hundred people for two intense and deeply meaningful hours at a panel discussion, "Gender: The Unnecessary Divide," sponsored by St. Luke's Methodist Church in Houston, Texas. All four panelists, experts in their respective fields, spoke eloquently and passionately about the issues of gender injustice and inequality. Each of them echoed the same opinion, based on their experience and careers in industry, social work, depth psychology, and academia.

Regardless of the progress that has been made in gender equality, the gender war has not gone away, but has gone underground where, as things do when they are pushed down, suppressed and repressed, it festers and emerges in violence, relational breakdowns, confusion, and chaos.

"There is still much work to be done," each panelist declared, and after each had responded to prepared questions and the floor was open for discussion, it was clear from the intensity of the questions and the solemnity in the room that everyone was serious about the problems related to the issues facing men and women in the workplace, homes and families, and, sadly, the church.

"Honey, everything you thought was nailed down has come undone," a woman told me when the local meat market closed.

Indeed, the institutions of marriage, home and family, organized religion, education, the legal system, medicine, and government as we have known them are all in an unnerving and disorienting sea change. How men and women relate to each other is no longer easily defined, smoothly carried out, or even understood by most people who are just trying to figure out how to make a living, forge a career, build a family, and stay somewhat safe and secure. That this is not my mother's world, or my father's, either, goes without saying, and there are days when I am thankful that my parents aren't having to flex and bend to the myriad changes in a culture they would no longer understand.

It is natural when things are in flux for us to attempt to find a firm foundation on which to stand, and often we regress to what used to work and what we know instead of being willing to lean into the fresh winds and new challenges of a world that challenges us to leave the past behind and press on into the future. Those who would attempt to return us to the Ozzie and Harriet television world of the 1950s or to a culture that denies the freedoms for all that have been gained are asking us to return to what would be a regressive, stultifying culture. And yet, in these sea changes, it's sometimes hard to figure out how to behave, what to say, and how to set appropriate boundaries and set each other free at the same time!

"I don't even know what it means to be a man anymore," a young, savvy man told me recently, "and I don't have a clue what women want!"

"Which woman? Which day?" I asked him, teasing, but he wasn't amused.

In response to the confusion and anxiety of our culture, there are those who would have us return to a hierarchical structure within the home and in churches. Still, there are denominations and churches that refuse to ordain women, either for the diaconate, the ministry, or the priesthood, and there are still religious groups that insist that women cannot lead because, they say, sin came into the world through a woman.

Only a few years ago, a young woman followed me back to my room one night after a session at a retreat I was leading on this subject. Standing in the shadows, away from the porch lights, this woman told me how her in-laws, members of a large church in my city, had forced her to sign a card stating that she would be submissive to her husband.

"Don't stop talking about this," she told me, looking over her shoulder to see if her friends were watching her. "I'm too afraid to speak up, and so you must speak up for us."

Another encounter with distraught parents only a few months ago rocked me to my core. They described a situation with their daughter, a bright, beautiful, and well-educated young woman, who is now under the domination of a church whose doctrines have a prescribed and narrow role for her and for her children. Weeping, they tell me things about this church that I can hardly imagine. They fear for their daughter's well-being. They grieve for the loss of the sparkle in her eyes and her own God-given freedom of choice. They are devastated at the loss of relationship with their grandchildren, a loss precipitated by a difference in opinion about the role of women and children in the family. I cannot ignore my friends' pain, and I cannot act as if this is Afghanistan; this situation exists in my part of the world.

The extent to which women have risen to leadership positions in almost every area of our culture is counterbalanced by the restrictions on women in other places and the outright violence and abuse toward women around the world, and what I know for sure is that when women are oppressed, men suffer, too.

Patriarchy, the dominance of masculine values, injures everyone because it is an imbalance. Patriarchy cripples men, women, and children, whether it is in church or school, business or politics, because it is overemphasizes one kind of strength to the exclusion of its opposite kind of strength.

The answer is not to swing to the other extreme, however, to another imbalance. *Women do not win if men lose, and men do not win if women lose* (and I have to ask—are relationships *competitions*?). Somehow, we have to work together for win/win solutions. We are interdependent, interconnected, and our lives are interwoven with men and women around the globe. What happens at the local level affects the global world; what happens around the kitchen table gets played out on the playing fields of business, commerce, church, and state. What goes on in the living rooms and bedrooms of our homes gets acted out, projected out, or played out in the school rooms and board rooms of the world.

When my youngest daughter, Amy, was in a four-year MSW/MDiv program at Baylor University and Truett Seminary in Waco, Texas, I took her to a conference at Harvard Divinity School. The conference title was "Religion and the Feminist Movement," and for three days we listened to strong and courageous women such as Rosemary Radford Ruether, Elisabeth Schussler Fiorenza, and twenty-five others tell their stories. It was an exciting, stimulating, and challenging event.

"I wanted you to see something out in the larger world, Amy," I told her during one of the breaks as we talked with women from all over the country. I wanted her to see beyond what might be limited and limiting practices within our own tradition, and I wanted to support her deep spirituality and her calling, however she wanted it to unfold.

"And what about *you*, Mom?" she asked me, pinning me to a wall with her question. "*What about your calling?*"

I remember stammering out some feeble response about how it was too late for me, but it wasn't too late for her, *but she would have none of my puny answer.* Her confrontation has haunted me since that day; I took it seriously.

It's hard for me now to realize the constraints in my own thinking. I came of age in an era and a culture when the women I knew believed that a man's time, his thinking, his ways, and his work were more important than a woman's. Today, when I hear a woman criticized or ridiculed because she has *ambition,* I have to laugh. The women of my generation had ambition, but we hung it on a husband whom we expected to do for us what we would not do for ourselves. A woman was supposed to support her husband's work and encourage his ambition, and that was that.

A pivotal moment occurred for me, however, in the early 1980s. I had invited Minette Drumwright to speak to the women's group at our church in San Angelo, Texas. At the time, Minette was working with what was then the Foreign Mission Board of the Southern Baptist Convention. Bright, beautiful, and articulate, Minette had been thrust into a new role following the death of her husband Huber Drumwright, the former dean of the seminary from which my husband and father had graduated. I could not have imagined how Minette's opening words would grab my attention and alter my thinking.

Minette began her weekend presentation by asking how many of us believed that our time was as valuable as our husband's. She pressed further and asked how many of us believed that what we did with our time, whether as a homemaker, a volunteer, or a professional, was as important as a man's work. Gently, but firmly, Minette knocked on the door of my unconscious, reflexive thinking and opened my mind to possibilities I'd never considered, so deeply enmeshed was my thinking, choosing, and doing in the ways of my small world. What is even more significant to me now is that no one in that room branded her either "radical" or "feminist." No one thought she was out of line for opening our minds.

Those of us who came of age in the sixties now laugh together at how bound we were by cultural mores. We absorbed the rules from our families and in the churches, schools, and culture in which we were formed. No one told us that our culture valued masculine strengths more than feminine strengths, but when the radical feminists began to rattle our cages about the oppression of women, it was hard not to wake up and begin to look around and notice inequities and imbalances. I was, however, turned off by the militant figures; extremists blind some of us to their messages with their behavior.

I grew up in a culture that insisted its little boys should not cry and taught them that real men look and act like John Wayne or, later, Rambo or the Terminator. Our culture tells males that they must compete and defeat, and even the ministers of the gospel of the Prince of Peace are some of the first to call for war and the first to try to silence those who would speak for peace. Ours is a culture that values external control by an authority figure, judges results, and gives rewards or punishment based on performance, achievement, accomplishment, and acquisition. This system of values has prevailed in the organized church for as long as I can remember.

For the most part, our culture devalues and underpays those who work at jobs that deal with issues of a person's soul such as education, the arts, spiritual growth, and the nurturing of the young. We have elevated science and technology over the humanities. Athletes who can win the big prizes are paid gargantuan salaries, while those who teach the young live on unbelievably low incomes.

On the day that Minette Drumwright opened my mind, I still believed that masculine modes of thinking, based on logic and fact, are "better" than feminine modes of thinking, based on intuition. Men—and women—are taught to silence or ignore their feminine modes of thinking and rely solely on their masculine modes.

"Think like a man, Charlene," my friend was told, "and you'll go places."

Charlene did go places, thinking like a man. But she didn't end up where she or her father expected—or hoped.

I also believed it was possible to be totally objective, rational, and logical and that a grown-up person *controlled his or her* emotion, instincts, and irrational intuition.

"Women are just so emotional," a male friend said to me, as if being "emotional" were a character flaw. I always think about his indictment of women and emotion when I watch an athletic event in which fans and athletes do all kinds of things that make me think they are expressing emotion! I hear politicians and radio pundits ranting and raving, and I wonder, "What is this if it isn't *so emotional*!"

"Why does he cry?" a man snarled about his son's weeping when his friend was sick. "Doesn't he know that real men don't cry?"

"Why won't he talk to me?" woman after woman asks. "I'm not trying to control him. I just want to connect with him!"

"He's way too dependent," another woman said about her son. "Real men don't need anyone like he needs people."

I have observed that both men and women reject and sometimes even ridicule feminine strengths, within themselves and in each other. In fact, women often carry that rejection of "the feminine." When that rejection is allowed and encouraged, everyone is deprived of something important and significant. With the denial of something as important as the feminine aspect of oneself, a necessary and vital part of one's personhood, that person is fragmented and broken. Without the freedom to develop and use both sides of one's nature, a person is like a one-footed duck, capable of swimming only in circles.

In making changes, it is important to start with oneself. Before I rush out and try to make societal or even relational changes, I do best by starting with my own life and allowing inner growth to ripple out into other areas. Instead of flailing away at the symptoms, those outward manifestations of inward conditions, it is important to begin with the cause, but I am obligated to start where I am, with what I have.

Wouldn't it be an amazing thing if the church, the Body of Christ, could empower men and women to set each other free from rigid role constraints, understand the differences that are inherent in human beings, and yet learn how to use those differences creatively and redemptively?

Wouldn't it be shocking for the church to begin living out the truth that we all are made in the image of God instead of locking one another in rigid, unworkable role constraints? What if churches moved to the front of the parade of human transformation and progress and led the way in helping people make healthy and life-giving connections with each other? What if we really did take seriously the teachings of Jesus, the Reconciler, within his church, instead of setting men and women apart in power struggles and conflict?

What if the Body of Christ on earth began to make a difference in stopping the abuse of women and children around the world?

If you read the Gospel narratives carefully, it seems Jesus related to men and women with a natural ease, giving both dignity and respect. What if we who call ourselves followers of Christ did the same? What would be the result? Would we foster the light of leadership in folks who might otherwise hide their lights under a bushel?

"Can't you see that we are doomed as women?" the young woman asked me, pointing in her Bible to Genesis 3 in which God pronounces the consequences Adam and Even brought on themselves by eating from the wrong tree.

"I don't start my theology there," I told the young woman, and I could tell I was going to have to work hard to hold her attention. It was almost as if she had been brainwashed to accept a theology that started with the Fall and ended with her being subservient to men.

"God set it up from the beginning," the young woman told me. "There's no way out of it, and that is why we should be submissive to our husbands. It's God's way."

"Wait a minute. Wait a minute," I said, taking the Bible from her and turning to Genesis 1.

"It all depends on where you begin," I said. "If you begin with the actions of Adam and Eve, as you have suggested, and take what God spoke as punishment for all persons for all time, we *are* doomed to repeat the same mistakes over and over."

I paused, waiting to see if she would be open to a new thought.

"I start with the Original Blessing," I told her. "You see, here it is in Genesis 1 where God created male and female *in his image,* and then he pronounced his creation good! When you start there, everything changes in how you relate to each other."

I paused, hoping that she would stay with me long enough to see my point of view. I hoped that somehow, the message of hope would penetrate the shame that she had cloaked around her mind.

The woman shook her head. "What do you do with this part about men having to labor and women having pain?" she said.

I tried to show her that this is the *description* of how things were going to be for Adam and Eve. I told her that I believe the words in Genesis 3 do not reveal how God designed things to be between men and women but are a description of the logical results of the actions of Adam and Eve, and, in a way, a statement that with consciousness and with maturing, things do get harder! We can't, after all, stay in the womb, the nursery, or the Garden forever!

I explained to her that the way Jesus treated women is instructive to us and that Christians must interpret all of the Bible through the centerpiece of our faith—the life and teachings of Jesus. She was shocked to hear that, but I was more shocked that she had been taught only part of Paul's message and that she had been taught to elevate the teachings of *Paul* over the life, teachings, and work of *Jesus.*

"God granted us free will," I said. "Having choice is our blessing and our burden, but God's attitude toward men and toward women from the beginning has been one of blessing."

At some point, we've got to grow up and accept the blessing of responsibility and the blessing of maturity, and maybe one of the ways we can do that is to begin blessing each other as men and women, made in the very image of God. Perhaps if we live from the blessing instead of the punishment, we might be healthier, happier people. Certainly, living from the position of punishment hasn't made us better people.

"What do you do with Paul's teachings?" the young woman asked me, defiantly. "Don't you think we should follow the Bible?"

"Which part?" I responded, and then I turned to one of my favorite verses, Galatians 3:28, and said, "You tell me first what you do with this one: '*There is neither Jew nor Greek, slave nor free, male nor female, for you are all one in Christ Jesus.*' Tell me," I asked, "why do you emphasize the teachings of Paul and not Jesus, especially since we are *Christians*?" I waited while she pondered her answer.

"I've not ever thought about it," she told me. "I guess I've just always believed what I was told at my church. It's really scary to think new thoughts," she admitted, "and it's scary to think for myself and to trust my own thinking!"

"What is scarier," I said to her, "is that this is a new idea for you. We've been in church a long time together, and we're only now talking about Jesus' view of all persons."

What is scarier than thinking new thoughts is clinging to the old ones when they no longer serve us and, in fact, destroy what is precious and sacred within human beings and between us.

"My daughter is leaving the church," my friend said to me. "She says that when she has to attend a church where women are marginalized and kept out of leadership, it violates her beliefs, her education, and her worth as a human being."

"My friends won't even interview for a church staff position if they find out the church refuses to ordain women," a young seminary graduate told me. And yet, still there are religious groups who take the opposite position.

What *would* Jesus do?

Indeed.

Perhaps what the Living Christ, the Holy Spirit, is trying to do through all of the restlessness related to gender, sexuality, and abuses of power is to get us to wake up and see what we have done to each other.

Maybe the time has come when we can start forgiving each other, releasing each other from the straitjackets of gender prejudice and bias, and granting each other the opportunity to learn new ways of being adult men and adult women in a culture that desperately needs adults to act like adults.

In the past few weeks, I've made a point of bringing up the subject of love in several venues among some sharp people who are intentional in their attempts to be responsible citizens and conscious human beings. Every time, I've been startled at how the subject of loving each other brings the conversation to a halt. Perhaps the silence I experience when I bring up the subject of love is about a collective awareness at some unconscious level that we have trivialized the word so much that we don't know how to talk about love very well. Or maybe just *talking* about love makes us feel vulnerable and exposed.

Maybe some of us carry within us, underneath everything else that is underneath, an awareness of our failures in loving each other well. Maybe we feel insecure about our capacity to love and our willingness to be loved, and maybe for some of us there is unbearable and sometimes unspeakable pain and shame and guilt about our mistakes in loving. Perhaps we know that we could have made a difference in someone's life if we had been able to say "I love you" better, and maybe the ways we have withheld love, given conditional love, or looked for love in all the wrong places feels so bad that we hate to open up and talk about it, especially to the people we say we love.

As I write these words, the season of Advent is only three days old. One more time in this season of long nights and short days, people all over the world will begin the annual remembrance of an event that changed the world. Wouldn't it be amazing if those of us who enter into this tradition and celebrate Advent become better messengers of *love?* Wouldn't it be interesting if those of us who call ourselves followers of the One whose birth we celebrate carried and expressed authentic love and goodwill in our workplaces and homes more readily and willingly than we carry the bad news of the day?

What might happen if we who celebrate Christmas considered ourselves under divine appointment to be the conduits of love to the crabby people we meet during the holidays, giving compassion and patience even to the people who irritate us? How could things be different if we chose to study the ways of love as carefully as we study the ways of war or the ways of politics? What would happen if we, as a culture, stopped trying to polarize each other around ideologies, hot-button issues, litmus-test theologies, and political positions? Does the "us versus them" language we hear in politics, in religion, in families, in cities advance or hinder our sharing the love of Christ?

And what better place is there to begin a new era of love than between men and women? It sets my brain spinning to think about the difference love can make; more important, it opens my heart and makes me vulnerable. Yes, that is scary, but angels and messengers of love really might be most active in helping those who are *willing* to love.

Questions for Reflection and Discussion

1. What are your prejudices and biases about what men should and should not do? What about women?

2. Are your prejudices your own, or did you inherit them?

3. How well are you prejudices and biases serving you?

4. How is your life, as a man or a woman, different from that of your parents? How do your parents feel about your choices?

5. Do you see or know about any abuses of power between men and women in your workplace, your church, your family, or among friends?

6. Is there any way in which you go along with gender bias and abuse by your silence? Could you help anything by speaking up or taking action?

7. Is what you want for the children in your life different from what you want for yourself, a co-worker, friends, or a spouse?

8. What is the most unfair thing you see in your world? Who is keeping that unfairness in place? Who benefits from the unfairness?

Taking Action

1. Make an assessment of the places in your life where you have influence.

2. Engage your friends or family members in a response to this question: What is the difference between loving someone because you need him or her and needing someone because you love him or her?

3. Ask the members of your church to evaluate gender equity within your church. Who is comfortable with the status quo, whatever it is? Who expresses discomfort with the status quo?

Just Don't Say Anything about It

The truth is that navigating your relationship by simply doing what "comes naturally" actually stacks the odds against achieving lasting happiness.

—Terrence Real

"This is my command: Love each other."

—John 15:17

The biblical revelation makes clear that Christ placed equal value upon females and males. In our day the Spirit is leading us toward deeper understanding and application of this truth.

—Jann Aldredge Clanton

When I was a young and in a situation in which I might say something that I shouldn't say, my mother had a gentle and gracious way of coming up behind me, slipping her arm around me, and pinching the tender flesh on the back of my arm.

"Just don't say anything about it," she would tell me quietly, and I would be quiet or change the subject, wincing with the pain in my arm and the fear of what might happen if I should comment on whatever it was that she wanted to ignore. "Just be quiet about it," I heard her say a zillion times, and now that I think about it, I realize she was still using the pinch and the silencing up into her eighties!

All the time she was pinching me, my mother would smile beneficently at whomever it was whose issue we were supposed to pretend we didn't notice. Who could have imagined that that sweet lady could be delivering the Killer Pinch and look so innocent! My sister said our mother was Margaret Thatcher, masquerading as Aunt Bea on *The Andy Griffith Show*.

So it was that in June 2007, as I was making my way down the three escalators of the Grand Hyatt Hotel in Washington, D.C., to lead a workshop on gender reconciliation at the annual assembly of the Cooperative Baptist Fellowship, I thought I could feel my mother's pinch on the back of my arm.

I was about to introduce my topic on gender reconciliation for the first time to my people and for the first time in several years. From previous experiences, I knew that no matter what, the topic would generate animated discussion.

Walking into my workshop, I couldn't keep from thinking about how in other parts of the world, these conversations about gender equity had been going on for decades, but I also knew that the issues dividing men and women were not resolved.

Gender issues touch us at our most sensitive, tender, and vulnerable places. In a culture where all of the institutions are experiencing massive changes and with the old roles and rules outdated and unusable, all of us, if we are honest, feel protective and sometimes defensive about being who we are in a world that no longer looks like the world of our parents. I recognize that the nervous twitters about "finding my feminine side" from men and the anxieties of women about their own roles mask deep feelings, and so I attempt to be gentle and respectful of the workshop's participants.

Having reworked my material to accommodate the current culture and now with a contract to write this book, I was curious to see what the response to my workshop topic would be. Would people come? If they did, would they be open and receptive? Could I effectively communicate this material through the inevitable defense mechanisms that make people hear only what they want to hear?

As the room filled, I was acutely aware that each man and woman who entered that room had a lifetime of experience, a ton of baggage, and, quite likely, some kind of wound that had to do with a gender issue. I knew that each one was bringing preconceived notions of what the workshop might be, prejudices, blind spots, confusion, biases, disappointments, and fears, and that one of the fears had to come from the confusion that results from trying to live with political correctness—something that often feels like my mother's pinch.

I knew that each person, including myself, would be coming from his or her own life experience and opinions about what it means to be a man or a woman in today's world. I hoped that each person would also bring an open mind and an open heart, a receptivity to new ideas, and a willingness to enter into the difficult process of learning something new, changing one's mind, or risking reaching out to the Other—the other side of oneself or the other gender—for the sake of wholeness.

Because my style of facilitating and teaching is often dialogical, I leave myself and the doors wide open for all kinds of reactions. People feel free within my classes and workshops to express themselves, and I encourage that. I also know that it is my responsibility to keep the container safe and steady so that learners can feel heard, validated, and respected. In general, there is typically lively discussion in my workshops and classes, and I like that!

In such an environment, and particularly with my topic, I knew that someone might say something that would offend another person. Emotions could flare, arguments could ensue, and peoples' feelings could be hurt. It was my job to manage all of that and manage my own feelings, for I, too, arrived at that workshop with personal memories of hostile reactions to this material! Managing my own fears and staying connected to my wild hopes for the workshop was part of my challenge. And I had to ignore the fear of the pinch from the portable mother complex who goes with me everywhere.

True-False "tests" are often a good way to engage a group in conversation and to discover where people are coming from when they show up in a workshop, and so I started with one. As I had expected, eliciting the responses to the following statements was all that was needed to stir up a lively conversation.

On that summer day in Washington, D.C., it didn't take five minutes for the lid to come off any self-restraint among the participants! Clearly, these people had an idea of what the masculine/feminine stuff had to do with everyday life, and they were eager to talk about it!

Here's the test I gave them:

True or False?
1. In the United States, the gender war is over.
2. Gender issues in the workplace are solved by legislation.
3. All persons have both masculine and feminine strengths.
4. Women are not competitive.
5. Patriarchy is damaging to both men and women.
6. Men are confused by what women want today.
7. An athlete's ability to cry over the loss of a championship is evidence that he is in touch with his feminine side.
8. The church has helped facilitate gender peace.
9. Women believe they know what men want.
10. Men and women are more alike than they are different.
11. A person should get a job only if he/she is the most highly qualified person for the job, regardless of gender.
12. One of the worst things to come from the feminist movement is the confusion about gender roles.
13. People often feel shame if they do not live up to the role expectations of their religious/social culture.
14. Women are shamed if they cry in the workplace today.
15. Men would rather die than show fear.
16. Feminism as a movement is dead.
17. Basically, men and women want the same things.

In their responses to the statements, both men and women revealed their prejudices and biases, their fears and frustrations, their wounds and their wishes, and it was up to me to keep alive an atmosphere of respect. At one point, emotions were running so high that I stopped the conversation and said, "I know this is difficult, but let's suspend our need to be right just for this hour and enter into the space of openness to new ideas and new possibilities." I could see the pain of failure and the fear of opening up to each other in that room of strangers.

In nearly three decades of presenting workshops on a variety of topics, I have learned that *nothing* is as guaranteed to stir up all kinds of interesting discussions as the topics related to female/male relationships. It is also my experience that in many ways, conversations about gender issues are more sensitive today than they were in the beginning; perhaps the pile-up of misunderstandings, abuses of power in the efforts to correct injustice, weariness from the tedium of balancing diversity in the workplace, and the ongoing confusion about gender roles has made us edgier and more sensitive with each other.

"To be honest, we just can't see what this masculine/feminine stuff has to do with everyday life."

I gripped the phone, unable to believe what I was hearing from my book publisher.

What was he *thinking?* Wasn't he reading the news? What did he mean, "this masculine/feminine *stuff*?"

Stuff?

This publisher had published two of my books, and in my naiveté, I thought that the company would want to be on the cutting edge with the book I was proposing. Though the topics of gender justice, gender peace, and gender equity were widely discussed in the larger reading world, Christian publishing wasn't flooding the market with anything about gender justice or gender peace.

And that was his point. They didn't see the relevance of my topic. It wasn't that the topic wasn't relevant; it was that *they* didn't see the relevance. Perhaps they thought that I should "just be quiet about it."

I put my outline in the filing cabinet and wrote three other books. I assumed I'd missed the moment.

On a summer morning in 1999, I walked briskly into the beautiful dining room of a country club where I was supposed to speak to a large group of professional women. Entering the room, I found the woman who had asked me to speak, and she led me to my seat. I had returned the night before from an eleven-day contemplative retreat at the Benedictine Monastery in Snowmass, Colorado, and so I was feeling refreshed, restored, and mellow. I felt confident and composed about my assignment for the morning.

For the first time since my former publisher had told me that he didn't know what "this masculine/feminine stuff" had to do with everyday life, I was presenting my material on that very subject to a large group of sophisticated professional women. I was excited and ready.

About mid-way into my material, though, a woman in the crowd stood and began to challenge me on my material. I paused and responded to her comment, attempting to respect her point of view and yet retain the focus of my speech. However, she only increased the intensity of her contradiction, both in volume and force. I tried to be gracious and understanding, but her angry vehemence unnerved and disturbed me.

Somehow, I managed to regain the floor, but I will never forget the tension in that room or the discomfort of the women sitting near this woman. Many of them later apologized to me for her behavior.

Later, I found out that the woman had fought hard to achieve her position in her particular field. What I knew for sure was that I had both touched a tender, frazzled nerve in her and that her behavior had proven several points I was presenting about what happens to women who overemphasize their masculine strengths.

After processing that incident and gleaning the gold from it, I filed the experience away. However, the memory came roaring back during the week after the April 2008 incident at the Fundamentalist Latter Day Saints compound in Eldorado, Texas. More than five hundred women and children were taken from the compound to shelters in San Angelo, Texas, after authorities received what they believed was a call reporting phyical and sexual abuse from someone living within the compound.

Listening to the NPR interview with one of the women who had earlier escaped the sect, I was riveted by something the woman said that evoked my memory: "Your listeners need to know that not only are the women abused by the men, but the *women* in the sect are abusive *to the other women.*"

In my speech to the group of professional women, I had emphasized that often women keep other women from gaining power. In an attempt to encourage women to become supportive to each other, I gave an example about how it is often women who are most cruel to other women. Showing how a person can move back and forth between masculine and feminine strengths, I emphasized the need for women to stop competing (often in covert and subversive ways) and start cooperating with each other.

After the interruption to my speech, I concluded with something I had never said before that morning.

"Many of you have succeeded in professions that were formerly unavailable to women. Many of you can no longer even imagine not being free to do whatever you want to do, go where you want to go, purchase what you choose to purchase or even believe and say what you want to say, but I know that there are women around the world and in this city who are not free, and as long as one of us is not free, we must keep on speaking out and speaking up about the things that bind others in systems of violence, abuse, and disempowerment."

Ten years ago when I responded to this woman who was so angry about what I was saying, I was really thinking about women in Third World countries. Fresh on my mind, as well, was a book my daughter Michelle had used for her master's thesis at Baylor University (and then urged me to read)—*The Handmaid's Tale*, published in 1985 by Margaret Atwood. In this chilling novel, Atwood describes the world in which women exist in a secluded home, controlled by men, and dehumanized by "the Commander" and his wife. The handmaids, who are used only for reproducing and running errands, are at the lowest social level, and other women frequently spy on them to report any perceived wrongdoing.

I could not have foreseen the current events in San Angelo, Texas, where I have deep and lifelong roots, as law enforcement and Child Protective Services deal with the challenges of a system so abusive and oppressive of women that it is even hard to listen to the details which grow more incredible and ghastly each day.

However, I knew intuitively and I knew from the experience of listening to women's stories for decades and from observing our culture that in spite of the advances made by some women in some places, the work of liberation is far from completed.

In light of what is unfolding as women coming out of the polygamist sects are willing to talk about what happens inside those compounds, it is fascinating now to read a comment from the back of Atwood's novel and published in the *Houston Chronicle*: "Atwood takes many trends which exist today and stretches them to their logical and chilling conclusions. . . . An excellent novel about the directions our lives are taking. . . . Read it while it's still allowed."

I repeat: *Women do not win if men lose, and men do not win if women lose, but when it comes to relationships, life is not a competition, after all.*

"What are you going to tell people about seeing *the movie*?" a young man asked me last year, and I asked, "What movie?"

"*The DaVinci Code*," he said, and I couldn't tell if he was challenging me, trying to trick me, or if he sincerely wanted guidance.

"I'm not sure I know what you're asking," I responded, puzzled, and then he told me that he had heard his friends talking about how he shouldn't see the movie. After all, the word was out from Christian talk radio that people should boycott the film.

I took a deep breath. In the first place, I don't dictate what movies people should or should not see, how people should vote, and what books should be banned. Just because I teach and write *about* God does not mean that I speak *for* God!

Taking seriously the question, however, I responded in the same way to this friend that I had responded to many others who had asked me the same question.

"It's my opinion," I told him, "that the outrage expressed from Christians about this novel and movie says more about us than it does the culture. The furor I'm hearing reveals a very low opinion of women, marriage, and human sexuality. We have a lot of growing up to do!"

"Besides," I added, laughing, "I wish someone would ban my books! That would guarantee their success!"

Indeed, *The DaVinci Code* broke all kinds of publishing records, and those of us who are writers and those of us who study the culture have to ask what that book evoked in the reading public. What about Dan Brown's fictionalized account of the life of Mary Magdalene made men and women of all ages read the book and talk about it with such intense interest?

Indeed, there are many answers to those questions, but I believe that part of the answer has to do with the fact that "the feminine"—feminine strengths, feminine wisdom, feminine gifts and abilities—has been neglected and maligned for a long time. This story engaged people across generational lines in discussions about ideas that I could never have imagined when my publisher told me he didn't know what the "masculine/feminine stuff" had to do with everyday life.

On a day last fall, I stepped into a car in New York City. As I buckled my seatbelt and got ready for the ride from 23rd and Lexington up to 110th and Amsterdam, the driver of the car said, "It's Gridlock Wednesday; it's a good thing we're leaving early."

Catching my puzzled expression in his rearview mirror, he said, "I don't know how those radio announcers know it, but every intersection I crossed coming to get you was in gridlock. I don't know if they know it's going to happen or if they make it happen!"

I was indeed fascinated by the gridlock at every intersection. Instead of cooperating with the traffic lights, cars and cabs piled out into the intersections together so that no one could move, and then, in what seemed to me utter absurdity, the drivers would start honking their horns, as if that would help! What I'd hoped would be a quick trip turned out to take twice as long as it should have.

"What a great metaphor of the world," I thought to myself, "especially the world of male-female relationships."

In today's world, men and women are all out in the intersections of life, honking the horns of blame and punishment at each other, trying to force the other person to do what we want him or her to do.

I do not have "the answer," but I can offer what I have learned from others who were able to point me in this direction or push me in that direction. What I have learned and experienced, I believe, could be one way out of the gridlock of gender conflict and into a smoother flowing traffic of peace, love, and justice.

I have learned that this masculine/feminine "stuff" has *everything* to do with everyday life!

Recently, I was in a conversation with Taylor Sandlin, friend, fellow pilgrim, and pastor. Born in 1978, he brought an interesting perspective from his generation and his college major in rhetoric to our discussion about the different ways women and men are perceived in our culture. "If a woman shows emotion," Taylor told me, "she is perceived as weak, but if a man does, he's considered to be compassionate. If a woman is strong and forceful in her communication, she is called names and described in unflattering terms. If a man is strong and forceful, he is considered authoritative and powerful."

It's not fair, but we can learn from the unfair parts of life.

At dinner parties or in casual conversations, when I am asked about this book project, the mere mention of the title has either brought the discussion around the table to a screeching halt and an uncomfortable silence, or it has elicited nervous laughter, instantaneous opinions about the topic (whether I've explained my point of view or not), or outright aggression against either men or women, depending on who has the floor.

More than once, a man or a woman has gone on a tirade, assuming that I'm writing from one perspective or another (the one he or she *hates*) without taking the time to hear either where I'm coming from or where I'm going with the project. As a listener of peoples' stories, I've learned to pay attention to the times when people speak from their pain; often, that pain is hidden behind anger, attack, and blame. Sometimes, though, a person speaks with simple clarity.

"I saw my dad develop his feminine side," Jason, a young man, told me. "It's almost like he got lost in that feminine side and lost something important in himself. And my mom became so fierce about being independent that I think she lost something real about herself! Maybe my generation can learn from our parents' mistakes but not give up the progress they've gained."

"Oh, my mother was liberated," a mid-life woman told me, speaking with deep bitterness. "She was so liberated that she's run off every man she's ever known, and she's about to run off my brother! Don't talk to me about women's rights!"

Interestingly, that brother had his own point of view. "I wanted my dad to stand up and be a man," he told me. "I wanted to see him strong and forceful and not just angry. I wanted him to show me that he could take care of himself and our world, but instead, he folded. He folded into his easy chair. He folded into his beer, and he folded into depression and we lost our dad."

Deep wisdom from young men and women always takes my breath away, and sometimes I cry. Such wisdom from young men and women has usually come with a price. There are casualties from the gender wars, and it is those casualties that reveal to us our growing edges, those places where we can learn and experience redemption.

This "masculine/feminine stuff" has more to do with everyday life than I could ever have imagined, and where there is the most pain and suffering, where there is the most injustice, abuse, and violence, where there is the greatest blindness, prejudice, and bias—*that* is where God is most likely calling those of us who label ourselves followers of Christ to partner together to stop the cruelty, right the wrongs, alleviate the suffering, open blind eyes, and set prisoners free.

I am convinced that God is right in the middle of suffering, begging those of us who are strong to help those who cannot help themselves.

At this point in my life, and with the life experiences I have had, I cannot be silent about this.

The stakes are too high.

It's worth the pinch.

Questions for Reflection and Discussion

1. What does "this masculine/feminine stuff" have to do with *your* everyday life?

2. In what ways are men and women caught in the gridlock of blame?

3. Do you agree that the outrage of *The DaVinci Code* reveals a low view of women, marriage, and human sexuality? Explain.

4. In what parts of your life do you feel that you have been discriminated against because of your gender? When have you discriminated against someone either because of your gender or because of theirs?

5. When was the last time you cried? Were you alone? What was the cause? Is it hard for you to cry?

6. When was the last time you felt joy? love? delight? How did you express those feelings?

Taking Action

1. Take a poll among your friends, asking the questions: Is the gender war over? Does anyone care about the gender war any more? Do you think you create gender war or gender peace with your behavior?

2. Gather a group of friends together, both men and women. Respond to the True/False statements together. Ask the group to draw three significant conclusions based on their responses.

3. Tell someone else about the concepts in this book, whether you agree with them or not. Send that person's response to the author at writer2530@aol.com.

How Big Is Your Fig Leaf?

If we can ever cut through the fog of projections in which we live so much of our life, and look truly at another person, we can perceive an ordinary creature as magnificent. The trouble is that we are blinded by our own projections; we rarely see another clearly in all of his or her depth and nobility.

—Robert Johnson

The man and the woman were naked, and they felt no shame.

—Genesis 2:25

Men and women in today's society are equally *wounded, in many different gender-specific ways, by a co-created culture that is equally sexist toward both. . . . The traditional gender roles of previous generations frequently imprisoned men and women in soul-killing routines.*

—Aaron Kipnis and Elizabeth Herron

The Lord *does not look at the things man looks at. Man looks at the outward appearance, but the* Lord *looks at the heart.*

—1 Samuel 16:7b

"Men are *jerks,*" a woman said as she wrapped the blood pressure cuff around my arm, "and women are *stupid.*"

And there you have it, I thought to myself as she pumped up the cuff and I pondered her words.

This particular acquaintance, one of the aides in my doctor's office, is always upbeat and positive, and so her comment surprised me. "I'm not the first person to say that," she said to me, perhaps noting my surprise.

We'd been talking about the ways young women hurt themselves by the choices they make when she made her pronouncement. I had this book on my mind, and so I pressed her to talk about what she meant.

How prevalent it is for us to label each other and ourselves, masking the uniqueness of our lives. We hide behind roles, personas, and images. We relate to stereotypes instead of *people.*

How is that working for us?

Ask a group of people to define God, and you'll get a roomful of ideas. There will be so many different definitions, in fact, that you may wonder if you are living in the same universe! To assume that we all mean the same thing or have the same picture in our heads when we invoke the deity is to live in delusion; all of us bring different ideas and images of God to the conversation and to the church, the mosque, or the synagogue—and to the voting booth. Our ideas about God, our labels and our images of God, can prevent us from knowing God.

We humans carry ideas and images about God consciously and unconsciously in our heads, and we project those ideas onto the actual God and think that is who God is. God made humans in his own image, and some have suggested that we have been returning the favor ever since, making God fit our images. It's called anthropomorphism, and we all do it.

How smart is that?

Offer any of our emotionally charged words or concepts in a group and see what happens. How people define and understand family, church, motherhood, and patriotism makes for interesting discussions that sometimes lead us to a deeper experience of connection, and sometimes split us apart in differences and the need to be right. Increasingly, hot-button issues can end friendships, polarize communities, and divide families, churches, and countries. We may be drowning ourselves in the murky waters of labels, roles, and stereotypes, all the time wanting and needing connection and community!

Ask a group of people to define or describe "a real man" or "a real woman," and buckle your seatbelt. In defining and discussing gender issues, we project our own conscious and unconscious ideas about men and women onto actual human beings.

Whatever the definitions, it is certain that what is spoken may come either from a knee-jerk reaction, long-held prejudices and pain, or deep and thoughtful reflection. How a person defines male or female may reveal either a defensiveness born of insecurity, a deep satisfaction with one's own gender, or a lifetime of conflict about issues that cut close to the bone.

We humans cannot *not* project our inner images onto others, but our projections do keep us from seeing each other as we really are. Our projections, revealed in the way we label others, the rigid role constraints we place on each other, and the stereotypes we accept as truth, say more about us than the one upon whom we hang our unconscious material.

In the beginning, Adam and Eve existed in a state of blissful innocence, symbolized by their nakedness. There was nothing between them to separate them. In their original state, they were able to be vulnerable, transparent, open, and available to each other. There was no shame tainting their responses to each other, and they had no need to hide behind defense mechanisms. *That* is the original Edenic experience!

Sometimes I wonder what would have happened if they had stayed in that original state. Could they have grown up and matured without doing what they did in defying God's instructions? I'm not sure any of us really grows up without separating from home and parents, and I'm confident that our ability to love God with freedom is impossible without the freedom *not* to love him.

Whatever was the original intention of the Creator, once Adam and Eve woke from their original innocence, they became conscious of themselves—*self-conscious*—and their sheer nakedness. In Genesis 3:7, Adam and Eve sewed fig leaves to cover their nakedness and their shame, and I have come to understand those fig leaves as symbols of our defense mechanisms, those behaviors and patterns we repeat, the masks we wear and the personas we create to hide who we really are, and our fears of being discovered as who we really are.

I especially like it that the writer of Genesis goes on to recount that God made garments of skin for Adam and his wife, providing covering for them even as he was pushing them out of their Edenic state. The image of God as Seamstress is a tender one for me.

Labels

Indeed, some people, both male and female, do act like jerks, and we are all are prone to stupid moments. We all fall short of who we are as people made in the image of God. The aide in my doctor's office was not the first one to make that declaration!

Months later, when I told the attendant in my doctor's office that I planned on using her words in my book, she said, "You know, I'm really working on not calling people names. I call myself a Christian; calling people names isn't what I want to do."

With consciousness come choice and responsibility. With responsibility comes change, one awakened person at a time.

When it comes to race and gender, we are increasingly careless and ruthless about slapping labels on others. I suppose we do this out of fear or a thirst for power or control, but we also do it because labels have become acceptable. We laugh at cartoon characters and comedians who ridicule and insult people. Gestures and language that were once off-limits in everyday society are now commonplace among children and adults, with people everywhere forgetting that how you talk to and about others says more about yourself than it does the other person.

Once we label someone, it's hard to see that person for who she or he really is. Labels allow us to dehumanize others, allow us to create distance between "us" and "them," allow us to judge others with an oversimplified criterion. When we attach labels to others, we become blind to who "those people" truly are.

Language such as "You can't trust him; he's a man," or "You know women; all they want is your money," demeans both the speaker and the subject of the derisive language.

Standing in front of a wall of children's t-shirts, sizes 3-6, I was appalled at the messages emblazoned across the fronts. Are the messages "Girls Rule; Boys Drool," "Girl Power," and "Eye Candy" appropriate for *children* to wear? Do we really need to fan the flames of the gender war from childhood?

"He's just a man," women say. "What can you expect?"

"Women!" a man said to me, rolling his eyes. "You're all just alike."

I bit my lip to keep from giving them my speech about how all people are unique. I assumed that it would have been wasted on them, but even my assumption is labeling, isn't it?

Roles and Images

"When you are introducing yourself to someone today," I asked a group of adults in a class I teach, "what do you use to earn credibility or make connections? What is on your personal résumé?"

Are you someone's (wife) (husband) (daughter) (secretary) (physician) (boss)? Which of your roles matter most to you?

Do you introduce yourself by profession? Does announcing yourself as the CEO, a PhD, the janitor, the favorite niece, or the preacher's kid get you in or keep you out? Does what earns you membership in one group keep you off the rolls in another?

Most of the people in my class had lived in Houston for many years, and so having to establish themselves as persons worthy of being known and befriended is a remnant from the past. One of our class members, however, opened our eyes to what happens when you lose your old, familiar roles or when life forces drastic changes.

"When I entered your world two years ago," Maryann Gerrity said, "I was learning to walk through a great loss in my life. Away from my old social circle, religious group, and friends and without any current work credentials, I had lost my résumé."

New to all of us, she really did not have *any* of the roles or personas that we rely on to give us identity and security when we are getting acquainted or establishing relationships. Reflecting on the way Maryann had made a place for herself among us, I am startled to realize what courage she had, bringing just her *essence* to us. Forced to make it on her own and without any role or image to protect her, what she presented to us was the sheer goodness of who she really is.

"Losing my fig leaves," she continued, "was my most important turning point to letting God clothe me. The one label I did come to this church with was *child of God.* Truly, it is the only label that will allow me to love as I was created to love. When we lose our fig leaves, we are as Adam and Eve were before they had to hide."

Who am I without my roles? How well would I function without them? What are my defenses when my image slips and people see parts of me that I don't want them to see? At the end of my life, will I be known for who I really am, at the core of my being, or only for the roles I played, the image I portrayed, and the masks I've worn?

While leading a women's retreat recently, I spent time talking to some of the participants. One woman said, "I almost didn't come because you are a *Baptist*," and before the weekend was over, others had said, "I came because you are a *Baptist*." Whatever their image of me, I am who I am, and what I long for is what every human wants. I want to be known for who I really am. I want to be accepted and loved just as I am.

When I look back on my narrow and small understanding of the roles of men and women when I reached adulthood, I shudder. In my youthful ignorance and without thinking about it, I operated with an unconscious image of what women should do and what men should do. I made decisions based on the rules I brought from childhood and my adolescent dreams, much of which were based on the romantic movies of the 1950s and '60s.

When I married, I happily assumed the role of *wife*, and I had a mental image of what that meant, an image formed from watching my mother and other women in my life, reading the women's magazines, and watching television and the movies! Out of that yet unconscious image, I set out to do what I believed a good wife should do. Looking back now, I chuckle to think about what conversations my husband and I might have had if we had said, "What do you think wives do?" I assumed, without talking to him, that the ideas and images I had in my head matched those in my husband's head, and I'm pretty confident that he assumed the same about me!

When I became a mother, I eagerly assumed the role of mother. Becoming a mother was, for me, a kind of ultimate arriving at a place I had always wanted to be. Fulfilling the roles of wife and mother have been indescribably meaningful to me; moving beyond the roles and relating to my husband and my children as *people* is an increasingly rich and rewarding experience.

What I did not know at the time was that when I took on those roles, I became lost in them and more distanced from my True Self. Adding the role of "minister's wife" to my line-up of roles had affected me enormously. I am forever grateful to the wise words of my friend, Sandra Hulse. Her words have been a light to me through the years, often beaming guidance to me when my path had become dark, showing me how and where to take the next step. "The best thing and the hardest thing you'll ever do for yourself is to be the person God created you to be," Sandra told me, "and the best thing and the hardest thing you'll ever do for this church is to be the person God created you to be." What she did not tell me was just how hard that balancing act was going to be!

At a very difficult time in my journey, I said to Sandra, "My faith is so weak right now." She quickly replied, "I know, but mine is strong, and you can lean on mine right now." Every woman, and certainly every mother and wife, needs a strong woman to come alongside her now and then and, as my mother used to say, "prop her up on the leaning side."

There are many problems about role-playing, but one of the most insidious is that we get so identified with the roles that we think the roles are who we are! We let our roles set unrealistic goals and standards for us, forgetting that we are ordinary mortals. Who can maintain the roles of Perfect Mother or Perfect Wife? And how do you define those, anyway?

In our families and organizations, we often assign roles. The Favorite Child, the Sick One, the Hero/Martyr, the Rescuer, the Scapegoat, the Victim, the Bad Seed are only some of the roles we assume, all of them hiding the person underneath the roles.

My ideas about how men and women were to act seeped into my mind from the religious, socioeconomic, and geographic culture in which I'd been formed. About the time I became an adolescent, I began to expand my ideas of role expectations from *Seventeen* magazine, movies, and my peers, and, looking back, I realize that I always fell short of the glossy images portrayed between the covers of magazines and on the movie screen. Later, *Ladies' Home Journal*, *Good Housekeeping*, and then *Cosmopolitan* provided the air-brushed images that always made me feel that I was lacking somehow. Nevertheless, I kept trying to live up to the idealized images I absorbed from my culture.

The women's movement was gaining momentum as I was beginning my life as wife and mother. While it seemed so disassociated and disconnected from my life, what I know now is that however we responded to that movement, there is no doubting that it has changed forever the way we perceive ourselves as women and men.

Because of my temperament and background, the culture in which I grew up, and my desires for a family of my own, I was focused on caring for my family, baking bread, and running carpools. I was doing what I wanted to do with my life; indeed, I was fulfilling my childhood dreams and I believed that what I was doing mattered. I could agree with the need for equal rights, but much of what I read and saw didn't connect with me until I had two important learning experiences.

Between the births of our second and third daughters, I had a miscarriage that rocked me to my core, physically, emotionally, and spiritually.

Perhaps it was the catalyst that moved me out of my girlhood innocence and illusions of invincibility and into a process of maturing. Shortly after the miscarriage, my husband I were invited to be trained to facilitate marriage enrichment retreats and workshops with David and Vera Mace, the cofounders of the Association of Couples for Marriage Enrichment.

During our training, David and Vera spoke about the resurgence of interest in marriages based on a hierarchical model. David spoke seriously about the effects of that model on the members of the family, and it was his opinion that when a person gets stuck in a rigid role identity, something in that person begins to die. When that happens, the whole family is deprived of knowing the authentic person. It was David's opinion that the hierarchical model of family life is damaging to everyone in the family and is a major cause of depression in women. "I've never seen it work well," he said. "It nearly always produces sickness in the family."

In the training, we were also introduced to the idea of a "rolling agenda," an agenda that was fluid instead of fixed, set not by the facilitators of the retreat, but by the participants in a cooperative venture. The Maces did not present themselves as "the experts," though they were that indeed, but as participants with us in learning and discovering. Neither did they classify their methods as "feminine," but they were masters of moving back and forth between lecturing and imparting information, a masculine modality, and dialogue, participation, and collaboration, all feminine modes.

For the next several years as my husband and I followed the Mace model in facilitating marriage enrichment retreats, the issue of gender roles—their impact in the changing forms of contemporary marriage patterns and the way those role expectations could be *negotiated* (a feminine quality)—was put on the rolling agenda of every event.

I am embarrassed now to recognize how fixed and rigid were my own roles, even though I knew instinctively that times were changing and that the keys for riding the rapids of change were flexibility and negotiation.

Gender role issues are not just about who does the housework and who earns the paycheck. Gender affects how we perceive ourselves as human beings, male or female, what behaviors are acceptable for a man or a woman, and which ones are not, what feelings and emotions a man can express, but a woman cannot, and vice versa. Gender is about the rules we brought from childhood and the myths that prevail in the culture, defining a "real man" and a "real woman," whatever that is.

In my lifetime, I have watched all the cultural rules about gender roles shift and change, and marriage has undergone massive change. I see my young friends having to deal with rough edges, unrealistic expectations they place on each other, and underlying resentments as they try to meet the challenges of running a home, managing children, balancing careers, and maintaining their own relationship. Often, what gets neglected is the primary marital relationship, which caves in under the enormous weight of modern life.

In work situations as well, gender issues simmer below the surface but are often masked by other presenting issues. Men and women alike are afraid of lawsuits and sexual harassment accusations. In some places, the gender war is simply ignored even though it seethes beneath the surface. We aren't where we used to be, but we aren't where we need to be, either.

I am so thankful that the role expectations for both men and women have shifted and changed so that men and women can become more fully human. I am thankful that we are learning how to employ the full range of human strengths so that women can develop skills and abilities that are natural to their own uniqueness and men can do things that express a fuller range of their talents and gifts. Released from rigid role expectations, we are all are less likely to be "jerks" or "stupid"!

More than twenty years ago, when I first began presenting this material, I was bold and excited about what could happen if these internal shifts could take place. Once, leading a women's retreat in Marfa, Texas, for strong, capable, and hardy women, most of them from families that had lived on the ranches in that region for generations, I could sense that these ideas were resonating with them. I knew, as well, that they would not tolerate anything that didn't seem authentic.

Finally, one of the women spoke up, and when she did, she shocked me. "You've just helped me see why my family is so troubled," she said, and the room became deathly quiet. "In fact, a lot of our families are troubled," she continued, looking around at her lifelong friends who were nodding in agreement.

"We women give lip service to the man's being the leader in the home, but at home, we're really the ones in charge. The men get to run things on the outside, but at home, it's different. We all just pretend that they are running things at home because that's the way we think it should be, and that's the way it's always been."

It is a problem, and it causes problems, when outer appearance and inner reality don't match up and are, in fact, at odds with each other. No one of us is, however, fully consistent, and no family has it all together.

Taking a close look at the roles we play and being honest about the times and places in which we hide behind an image or a role helps us let go of baggage, inauthenticity, and role-playing and moves us into the wider spaces of freedom and grace. Beyond any role we play or beneath any image we want to portray is a real person, and the more we can be that natural and authentic person, the better everything goes.

I highly value my roles as wife and mother, but what do I do when my children no longer need a full-time mother and my husband isn't around? When there is no need for me to play one of those roles in the course of a day, there is more to me than the role!

"I don't know who I'll be when I'm not a teacher anymore," an older woman told me. "I've been a teacher so long that I don't know if I have any identity apart from my career."

Who hasn't known the executive who neglected every part of his life but his role, only to collapse and die the week after retiring? What happens to the femme fatale when her beauty begins to fade, depriving her of the image that she thinks is her identity? Hiding behind the roles we play in life, the images we have constructed to protect our insecurities, the positions that have given us status, power, and access can become a prohibition against living our authentic lives. Hiding always creates separation and isolation; openness, transparency, and vulnerability build connections and community.

What if our perceptions and pictures of how a woman is to behave keep us from being who God created us to be? Insisting that a person conform to the cultural stereotypes of maleness and femaleness makes us miss the gift of who that person really is.

Stereotypes

"I have been very happy, very rich, very beautiful, much adulated, very famous, and very unhappy."

It was Brigitte Bardot, designated a "sixties sexpot," who uttered these words, revealing the angst beneath the glamour of a cultural stereotype.

It does no good to argue that she benefited from her stereotype. The truth is that our culture seems to need various stereotypes, and there always seems to be someone ready to fill the need. Cultural stereotypes both reveal symbiosis and perpetuate it, as do the ones we carry in more personal ways.

When we stereotype others, we tend to use the terms "always," "all," and "never" to indicate that we have locked someone in to a particular image. Sentences that begin with "*All* women (or men) . . ." or "Men (or women) *never* . . ." should warn us that we are relating to a human being as an object—rather than a person created in the image of God.

"My husband's children cannot see me for the person I am. I will forever be the wicked stepmother to them," a friend told me. Families, locked in the straitjackets of stereotypes, injure each other over decades.

Sometimes it seems as if certain roles fall more easily into stereotypical behavior. Consider the qualities that are often associated with these "types": the televangelist, the adolescent or the old man, the troubled child, the "typical" patient, the mother-in-law, the starlet, the star athlete. The truth is that stereotypes aren't only perpetuated from the outside; some people internalize their roles and begin to act the part they think others expect of them. Who, then, bears the responsibility when the *authentic* person is all but invisible?

"You can do anything you want to do, Jeanie," my dad told me often, as I was moving through high school and college, "*but always be a lady.*"

He said those words to me many times, and he brought up the possibilities of my going into banking or law, professions that were largely male-oriented when I was coming into adulthood. Looking back, I think how radical it was for him to hold out those options for me when most of my peers went into teaching or nursing. What my father was doing was giving me permission to color outside the lines of the life script for a female in my culture.

Would that *all* young people had someone to expand their vision beyond whatever limits them and to open their minds to all of life's possibilities. Would that they, male and female, could have a strong internal voice guiding them out of limited and limiting belief systems and old scripts into the fullness of their potential.

Now I know, however, that the second part of Dad's message had greater force for me than the first part. "Being a lady" was *really* important in my religious and cultural world. There were *names* for women and girls who broke the rules or the stereotypes or who played a role outside the boundaries of what ladies were supposed to do, and I carried an unconscious fear of being ostracized or criticized for venturing beyond the boundaries of acceptable female behavior. I had no idea how much my father's words had at an *unconscious* level.

Though no one had ever given me a manual to help me know what that meant, I picked up the rules for being a lady from the time I was a little girl, absorbing them from the men and women in my world. I knew exactly what the rules were for being a lady: Be nice. Take care of your family. Be modest. Don't be coarse. Speak softly. Put others first.

Following those words to the letter, I would indeed have become a stereotype, cutting off the vital life force and uniqueness within me in service to the rules of my culture.

Perhaps it was the "Nice Person" stereotype that did some of the greatest damage to my emerging personality and wobbly sense of self.

The religious world in which I grew up did not make a big deal about women's roles because the roles were fixed and people lived obediently within them. Men simply *were* the leaders, and that was an unquestioned reality.

My father, a conservative Baptist minister, held traditional views about what men should do and what women should do, both at home and within the church, but he also said on numerous occasions, in both private and public, "If it weren't for the women, the church would have died a long time ago." In his ministry, he highly valued the investment of women in the life of the church and was deeply respectful of women's gifts. Repeatedly, he expressed pride in my sisters and me, always encouraging us to achieve and accomplish what we wanted to do.

My father's permission for his daughters was different from the expectations he had for our mother, but for a man of his time and his upbringing, he had an unusual sense of openness about what was possible for us. Furthermore, he was fiercely protective of his daughters.

My father was horrified by men who were heavy-handed with their wives or children and could be brought to tears by a woman or child in whose eyes, as he put it, the lights had gone out. From him I learned an aversion to using biblical teachings that were intended for the era in which they were written to "keep women in their place." Now I know that when the rules about the relationship between men and women are communicated within a religious context, invoking God to keep people in their proper place, there is a particularly damaging effect.

Those who use religion or the Bible to oppress the life force and the natural design, temperament, or calling of individual human beings are trespassing in realms that belong only to God. Much of what has been done to both men and women, but particularly women in my religious culture, has had the same effect on our souls as binding the feet of women in other cultures.

When you are locked into a role, whether you are a man or a woman, you are living what James Hollis has called "lives too small for our souls," and when that happens, our souls shrivel up in religious bindings that are as death-dealing as the wrappings that bound women's feet.

For decades, I thought my father was sending me a mixed message, and I wrestled with what he meant, sometimes thinking he had put a crimp in my style with that "being a lady" injunction. I realize now that what my dad was saying had a profound value and truth to it. For a man of his generation, he was acutely aware of the value of living out of one's natural strength. What he knew to say was, "Always be a lady," but what he meant was, "Don't lose who you essentially are."

Looking back, I know now that my father was ahead of his time. He knew that women who lose touch with the feminine strengths lose something important and vital, and he also sensed, I think, that feminine strengths were losing value in our culture. I think my dad saw that some women were overusing masculine strengths, to their own detriment. In fact, recent readings in the area of women's health and what is happening to women who adopt masculine strengths and neglect their own bodies and feminine strengths support my dad's intuition and deep wisdom.

When I was sixteen, and maybe before, I felt something stirring in my young soul, a stirring toward God. Wisely, my dad advised me to stay open and see what unfolded.

When I was about to graduate from college, I said to my roommate in a youthful burst of idealism and passion, "I don't necessarily want riches, but I want my life to count for something."

Now I understand those moments as holy moments, moments when I experienced a *calling.* Little did I know that following my calling, as a woman of my age, with my values about family but most of all with the constraints of my religious culture, would be one of the most difficult and painful conflicts of my life. I would spend decades being pulled between what I longed to do with that calling and the restrictions of my religious world.

I will be forever grateful for the ways in which I have been given to express my calling and for the people who have encouraged, supported, and believed in that calling. I am deeply grateful for the support, encouragement, and belief in me that my husband and daughters have given me as I have stumbled toward maturity.

Only days before my dad died, my sisters and I were having a spirited conversation with him about the changing roles of women in the church.

"How would a woman know if she is called into ministry?" my dad asked, and my sister quickly responded, "Well, Daddy, how would a man know?"

A look of surprise and amusement swept over his face and he laughed at himself. "Well, *of course*," he responded, "a woman would know in the same way a man would!"

What a gift it is to be able to change your mind at eighty-five! My father was a "man's man," and he had equal access to his laughter and his tears. He was a man who had taken good care of what had been entrusted to him with masculine strengths, but he was also able to flex his feminine side with natural ease and grace when needed.

When I reflect back on the way I perceived "how men are" and "how women are," I am appalled at my limited and limiting thinking. I had an absurdly narrow view of what roles a man could play, and in my culture, when a man stepped outside the traditional roles that were assigned to men, it didn't play well.

Where the women's magazines left off, interpretations of the Bible took over, and those who had an idea of how a woman should live stood on the writings of Paul with great authority. Women were to stay in their place, and their place was the nursery or the kitchen, and when they dared to step outside that culturally acceptable place, they were shamed and blamed for what happened to the children, the failures of society, and the breakdown of the family!

I know now that the stereotypes religion imposes don't have a thing to do with the freedom Jesus brought to us. Indeed, the rigidity of "the patriarchy" has overvalued masculine strengths and undervalued feminine strengths, to the harm of all of us. To use God and God-talk or the Bible to hold human beings down or back has to be one of the most sinister ways we take God's name in vain.

The lament, "What do women want?" should perhaps be turned inside out. Perhaps we need to ask the question, "*What is it we want from women*?" Indeed, each of us has expectations for how women are "supposed" to behave, and those expectations come from our personal histories.

If we observe our culture, it's hard to look away from the likes of Britney and Paris, Anna Nicole and Lindsay and take a long look at strong and capable women. We elevate the Virgin Mary and Mother Teresa to iconic status, but who among us ordinary mortals can live up to those archetypes? If we are honest, we all want an Eternal Mother who will continue to feed, nurture, and take care of us in the way we want her to, but leave us alone when we're tired of her! And some want a windup toy, a Barbie doll, cute, adorable, and adoring, a trophy or eye candy to enhance their own feelings of self-esteem.

Indeed, the rules about what it means to be a woman and what it means to be a man have changed, and life outside the box can be, by turns, exhilarating and terrifying. Without the rules that gave us structure and stability, we are in an awkward stage of development, individually, and the awkwardness certainly affects how we relate to each other.

One of my favorite scenes in the Old Testament is in Genesis 16 when Hagar, pregnant with Abram's child, had run away because of the jealousy and wrath of Sarai, Abram's wife. The angel of the LORD found Hagar near a spring in the desert, and after the angel tended her, Hagar said to the LORD who spoke to her, "You are the God *who sees me*." To be seen, acknowledged, known—that is the gift of love.

A wife, sobbing with the frustration of trying to be seen for more than her roles of laundress, cook, chauffeur, and nurse by her family, said, "I am more than this. I am a *person*, but you treat me like an object."

And if her husband were honest, he would confess that at times he, too, felt like an object: an ATM machine, a slave to his children, and a cog in the wheel of his company.

Perhaps it is time for each woman and each man to ask, "What do I want for my own life?" and "Who am I, really, besides my roles?"

Women and men alike ultimately give an account for their stewardship of their unique lives.

Artificially contrived diversity, forced processes to create the appearance of equality, and laws governing rights, employment, and harassment do not make the underlying prejudices go away.

Life is complex; relationships are difficult and demanding. To any encounter with another human being we bring our projections and biases, prejudices and needs, expectations, hopes, and fears. We bring our history and all our prior experiences to every event.

When I can live out of my own center of uniqueness, as a person created in the very image of God and only a little lower than the angels, I will not allow another person to reduce me to an object or role or stereotype, nor will I do that to another. I will not allow another person to use me or abuse me, nor will I use or abuse another. If I can hold this center of conviction in my everyday interactions, I can not only change my relationships, I can change my world.

If we can remember that every encounter with another person is an exchange of gifts, we will move beyond the labels and meet each other first and foremost as individuals created in the image of God. Remembering that we are all created in the likeness of God, we will be compelled to treat others with respect and dignity, allowing them to be who they are instead of who we think they are or should be. Our fig leaves will fall away.

One by one, we can make peace with each other, and as we make peace in our primary relationships, that peace will ripple out and out and out into the larger world.

Questions for Reflections and Discussion

1. Have you ever been called a jerk or told you were stupid? How did that make you feel? Have you ever called someone a jerk or "stupid"? How do you think that made that person feel?

2. In what role do you feel most comfortable? When you aren't in that role, how do you feel?

3. How do you want others to perceive you? How do you respond when someone perceives you in a different way from the way you see yourself?

4. How do you introduce yourself to strangers? What are the five things you want others to know about you? What are the things you don't want others to know about you?

5. What role did you play in your family of origin? Are you still trying to play that role now? How is that working for you?

6. What is the most liberating message you received about yourself as a man or a woman from your family of origin? the most limiting?

Taking Action

1. Take an inventory of your behavior and attitude toward the persons closest to you. Are you holding someone hostage to a label, a role, or a stereotype? What is the pay-off for doing that? Make changes. Now.

2. Are you holding yourself hostage to an old role, a label from childhood, or an unrealistic image you are trying to keep in place? Make a list of the ways that is depleting your energy. Make amends to yourself.

3. Give up labeling others. Don't announce it. Just do it.

What Lies Beneath

How can we be authentic when we are desperately trying to manage and control how others perceive us? How can we be honest with people about our beliefs and, at the same time, tell them what we think they want to hear? How do we stand up for what we believe in when we are trying to make everyone around us feel comfortable so that they won't get angry and put us down? It is impossible to be "real" when we are ashamed of who we are and what we believe.

—Brené Brown

And they were naked . . . and they were not ashamed.

—Genesis 1:25

"Shame is our most primitive emotion. It is pervasive throughout all cultures and with all persons."

The instructor who said these words was Brené Brown, professor in the Graduate School of Social Work at the University of Houston, a shame and empathy researcher, and author of the book *I Thought It Was Just Me: Telling the Truth about Perfectionism, Inadequacy and Power.*

"Shame and empathy are on two ends of a continuum," she stated, "and the more shame you have, the less empathy you have."

Of course! I could feel a "Yes!" resonating through my whole body, and my mind began to connect the dots between Dr. Brown's lecture and my writing project.

From Dr. Brown's work, I learned vital truths about the force of shame:

- Shame is best defined as the intensely painful feeling or experience of believing that we are flawed and therefore unworthy of acceptance and belonging.
- Shame often creates feelings of fear, blame, and disconnection.
- Rigid cultural definitions of women and their roles create shame in women. Likewise, how we expect a man to be, look, and act, our expectations, fuel shame in men.
- We cannot become shame resistant, but we can develop shame resilience.

As men and women, we use our labels, roles and images, and stereotypes as fig leaves, covering our shame. At a very deep level, the soul level, we need to reconnect with each other, and to do that we must develop our *joining forces—our empathy, vulnerability, compassion, and cooperation.* What lies beneath our seeming problems with each other must be addressed at a deeper level, the inner world where we crouch and hide in fear of being exposed.

"I don't think I have any shame," I've been told. Indeed, it is sometimes hard to see that this most primitive feeling lurks beneath our conscious minds, lying in wait and feeding us lies about who we really are. It is the nature of shame, in fact, to hide, and shame makes us hide from each other.

"Why are you writing this book from a spiritual point of view?" someone asked me. "Why bother with what is going on in the church? What does religion have to do with gender issues, anyway?

I love it when people challenge my ideas (well, most of the time!) because in the dialogue, I always learn something new, or in response to the demand that I articulate my thoughts more clearly, I come to understand what I believe and think more clearly.

"I'm speaking from within the system that I know best," I said, "but the truth is that I am convinced that gender is at the heart of our spirituality. How we believe and feel about ourselves as men and women with masculine and feminine traits is foundational. It is a spiritual issue, and the religious structures have a responsibility and an opportunity to set people free."

I could feel myself warming to my topic with passion and intense conviction. "It is religion that often perpetuates the wrongs against women, and I think that it is our obligation to stop the dysfunctional patterns of the centuries that we couch in religious terminology!" When wrongs are committed against other human beings in the name of God, aren't we taking God's name in vain?

"Women cannot be in ministry," the speaker at the microphone said, "because sin came into the world through a woman."

"*What did he say*?" I asked my husband. "Did he say what I think he did?"

"Don't worry about it," my husband said. "Resolutions aren't binding on a local church." We are, after all, Baptist, and we pride ourselves on the priesthood of every believer, the autonomy of the local church, and the voluntary cooperation with other entities. Resolutions, historically, represented opinions expressed by messengers, not delegates, to the annual meeting of the Southern Baptist Convention.

When I heard these words, we were sitting in one of the business sessions of the annual meeting of the Southern Baptist Convention in Kansas City, Missouri. It was 1984 and I was deeply involved in my own traditional life, raising my three daughters and keeping busy as a wife and minister's wife. Even if the resolution were binding, I didn't see how it would affect my life; I was, however, appalled at the rhetoric about the resolution.

Between sessions, I was reading Scott Peck's watershed book on evil, *People of the Lie*, and at the time of the discussion on the resolution about women, I was actually reading the chapter on religious evil. Only in retrospect did I catch the irony of the coincidence, but from that moment forward, I would have a new sensitivity to the ways in which life is destroyed by evil. Over the following years, I would come to an increasing understanding of the insidious ways in which religious evil operates, often masquerading as "good" and "goodness."

No one I knew, *or so I thought at the time,* would agree with the resolution, nor did I have any idea that the resolution and the discussion about it in that convention hall would come back to me over and over until I finally faced it and worked with it. What I also did not understand at the time was the way shame and silence had operated to keep women in their place for centuries.

Neither did I know at the time what that experience was doing to me, but years later I would realize that that moment could not have been more toxic for me. It was as if I inhaled poisonous fumes that permeated my whole psyche, creating pockets of insecurity and feelings of inadequacy, hesitancy, and outright fear of presuming to do what was in my heart, mind, and soul related to my gifts and talents. Hearing *authority figures* make a resolution that so denigrated women was a blow to my courage and confidence, but I did not know how powerful that blow was until years later. I suppose it was too painful to allow into my conscious mind.

Is there any way to account for the ways that belief about women would seep into the minds and hearts of girls? Did anyone stop to think about what messages that resolution would make to boys and men, and how that belief would seep into their relationships with women? Did anyone consider the fact that the resolution would be used as a weapon in the hands of people with selfish intents, small minds, childish fantasies, hard hearts, or cruel motivations? How can we measure the impact of that shaming declaration? What gifts of women have been lost to us because women were put in "their place"—a place defined by a flawed religious concept? Is there any way we can undo centuries of damage caused by the belief that women should stay in "their place"?

Time and life moved on for me from Kansas City, and a lot of people ignored that resolution, made fun of it, or left the church altogether. I was asked to be on the national Coordinating Council of CBF where there was a conscious, deliberate, and intentional effort to include women. The push for diversity was not easy. It went too fast for some and too slowly for others, but the overarching agenda was for inclusion.

I stand on the shoulders of fine men who advocated for the ministry of women both in my spiritual life and in my vocation as a writer and speaker. I will always be indebted to the men who put their own reputations and careers on the line to give a boost to women, and to the women who were courageous enough to step forward and claim the calling that God had for them.

I will always have the deepest respect, admiration, and pride at the way my husband led our church in San Angelo, Texas, in the ordination of women as deacons. It is one of the memories and realities I treasure most in our life together.

After a yearlong education process, my friend Delores Flood was ordained as the first woman deacon in Southland Baptist, and it was a glorious occasion. The education process was not without its bumps, but the whole experience was full of grace and optimism, hope and love.

The next year, another friend, Sybil Holveck, was ordained. At the appropriate time, my husband asked those in the congregation who wished to do so to come to the front and bless her with a touch of hands and words of affirmation. To our surprise, the children, most of whom Sybil had taught in Sunday school and Vacation Bible School, began to pour down the aisles, going to their teacher and friend, placing their young hands on her head and stooping to pray for her. I'm sure there was not a dry eye in the house that night. That everyone in that church, including the children—especially the children—felt valued enough to bless this new woman deacon still makes chills run down my spine!

In the late 1980s and early '90s, however, times were changing and a new resurgence of conservatism in the country and within church life had created a lockdown in areas that had been experiencing the fresh winds of the Holy Spirit. Those of us who had experienced gains by women in our churches and certainly in the secular world were shocked to see young women who were benefiting from those changes move back toward positions that would keep women stuck in anachronistic patterns.

I was shocked, as well, to hear echoes of the resolution that was passed in Kansas City in statements that were whispered and sometimes spoken with rage and disrespect. What I experienced, most of all, was a fear of change and a fear of women that felt irrational, outmoded, and suffocating. Nevertheless, I live in my culture, and I had to get along and go along with the prevailing rule, or so I believed.

In spite of the cultural turmoil within my religious world, increasingly I was asked to teach and speak and lead retreats about issues related to spiritual growth, prayer, and meditation. I was trained to do spiritual direction at the Spiritual Direction Institute at the Cenacle Retreat Center in Houston. I served on the Spiritual Formation Task Force and the National Coordinating Council of the newly formed Cooperative Baptist Fellowship, wrote books and columns, taught Bible studies, wrote Bible study curriculum, was trained to facilitate Centering Prayer groups, and kept a busy schedule leading retreats and workshops, speaking for various events, and sometimes even "filling the pulpit" at various churches on Sunday mornings. I've never quite been able to say that I "preach," a fact that annoys my family.

My world expanded more and more as I led events for men and women in Episcopal, Methodist, Presbyterian, and Lutheran churches. I was honored to be asked to lead a Bible study at a Church of Christ, and I loved the fact that there were women from all denominations in the weekly Bible studies I facilitated. I am honored to have Jews, Muslims, and Hindu friends who attend some of my classes, and I love leading retreats at the Cenacle Retreat Center, a Catholic center where people of many different religious beliefs and some who are struggling to believe experience the Presence of the Living God.

Looking at my life, no one would ever imagine that I was not living out the calling I'd experienced as a young girl. No one would have thought that I was not exercising my gifts, but the truth is that the resolution and the rancor in the convention center the day it was passed was somewhere down in my memory bank, waiting to be faced. It was festering there as something I hadn't imagined—as *shame.* I lived constantly with the feeling that I was doing something I wasn't supposed to do.

In the waning light of a December afternoon, just before the shortest day of the year and the coming of Christmas, I sat with one lovely woman with whom I do spiritual direction while she described a recent incident that had evoked deep shame in her. Listening to her describe the various characters in the situation, what they said, and then how she had felt, I found myself reacting with strong feelings. My feelings and my identification with her rather public experience of being shamed were like static in my head.

"*You* aren't the one who should be ashamed!" I said, surprising myself with the force of my reaction. "*They* are the ones who behaved badly! Why are you carrying the shame?" I asked.

We talked about why she was carrying the shame, and how women sometimes take on the shame or guilt that really belongs to other people! I told her about a time when I was teaching the Twelve Steps of Recovery in my Thursday morning Bible study and had an epiphany. Listening to the questions from the women in my class, I was distressed at the fact that they were carrying the burden of what other people had done, while the people who had done the harmful deeds didn't seem to realize how their behavior had affected other people!

"When you pick up the blame for what others have done and spend your life trying to atone for other peoples' sins, that is codependency!" I had declared with passion.

When I have such strong feelings about what I'm hearing from another person, I know to go within to try to separate my issues from another's. Finally, I had to tell her why I was so into this story.

"I've had a deeply shaming experience," I told her. "I have a sense of what you experienced."

"Tell me about it," my friend said, and so I did.

In 1999, I was asked to share the leadership of a retreat with a prominent religious scholar and leader at a place that had been a vitally important, sacred location for me for much of my adult life. I was honored to have been asked to co-lead this retreat, and while I had some anxiety and nervousness about it, I was looking forward to the experience with great expectation.

As I drove across Texas in the August heat to the event, all of the voices that sometimes taunt and intimidate me began their usual routine.

"Who do you think you are, a *woman*, doing this?" "You should be staying in your place, don't you know that?"

I knew I could do what the leaders of this retreat center had asked me to do. A part of me felt confident and secure in carrying out my assignment, but other tired, old, familiar voices were laying a huge load of bad feelings on me. At the time, I wouldn't have identified my feelings as shame; only in retrospect did I understand what they were.

On the second night of the retreat, the co-leader and I were to field questions and respond to subjects the participants had written on 3 x 5 cards. I felt uneasy for some reason; perhaps it was that this leader and I had not connected with each other yet. I was disappointed because I have great respect for this man and, besides, I wanted to please him and the people who had invited me to be co-lead the retreat.

As we perched on two stools in front of the crowded room, he handed me the 3 x 5 cards.

"Here," he said to me. "You can hand me the questions."

Looking at the first question, I caught my breath. I couldn't believe my eyes! Quickly, my decision of how I would be and behave was immediately challenged. *Is it O.K. for a woman to pray aloud in church?*

I stared at the question, unable to comprehend that at the end of the twentieth century, this question would even be an issue in what I thought was an enlightened crowd! As I said, I had put that Kansas City moment far behind me, but apparently others had not! While I had gone about my life, other people had bought into that belief represented by the Kansas City resolution. I put that question at the back of the stack of cards, but each question in my hand was as startling. There was nothing I could do, I thought, but hand them to my colleague as they came. I handed him the first question, written on the card that I'd put at the back of the stack.

I honestly believed in that moment that he would say, "Of course a woman can pray aloud in church."

For several minutes, however, my colleague spoke about how a woman could pray aloud in church *if she stayed in her proper place.*

The longer he talked, the more astonished I became. Slowly, I turned toward him on my stool, holding my breath in utter disbelief at what I was hearing, but more at the thought that I was going to have to answer that question, as well. To my left were the faces of people who were important to me, authority figures I wanted to please, and to my right, a friend and fellow traveler in the religious world, a man with an open mind and a big heart. Later, reflecting on that terrible moment, it seemed to me that the persons to the left and to the right of me represented the choice that was being demanded of me.

I could either people-please or be authentic.

I could either lie or tell the truth.

I could either die or live, and it was that serious.

Finally, my colleague said to me, "What do you think, Jeanie?"

"I have lived my whole life in the religious world you have just described," I began, and the room became deathly quiet. "But my father, a conservative Baptist minister, taught me that I could be anything I wanted to be, and besides, my experience of the Living God in prayer has been so powerful that . . . don't you think that sort of puts me on the horns of a dilemma?"

For the first time, my colleague turned and looked at me, and then quickly began to invoke the Bible. "I think we should stick with the Bible and what the Bible says, don't you?" he asked.

Months later, I was told that in my response that night, I was offensive. I believe I was authentic and truthful.

As I have reflected on the role of women in the church over these last three decades, I am still amazed at how our cultural conditioning and our personal biases inform our interpretation of the Scriptures. When it comes to those interpretations, I am continually surprised at three things:

I am surprised that people elevate the teachings of Paul over the life and teachings of Jesus. If we are attempting to be followers of Christ and if we call ourselves Christians, shouldn't the centrality of Christ inform both the Old Testament and the writings of Paul?

I am surprised at the ways in which we flawed and frail human beings pick and choose which portions of the Bible we will interpret in its cultural and historical context and which ones we prefer to impose onto today's culture. We humans tend to want to take literally that which serves our own purposes, purposes that may be totally outside our conscious awareness, but ignore those that don't!

I am surprised at how much we human beings look to the Bible to find rationale for our own points of view rather than letting the Bible speak for itself. I'm also surprised at how much biblical illiteracy there is among church members and how little the actual life and teachings of Jesus, the founder of our faith, are known among Christians. I wish sometimes that we would read and study the Bible with the same passion and zeal we give to fighting about it.

What is sad to me now, looking back on that hot August night, is how scared, humiliated, embarrassed, ashamed, and belittled I felt in my room after the session. Sadder to me was the way significant people shunned me and talked about me at the lunch table the next day, as if I couldn't hear what they were saying. I was shocked to learn sometime later that I had been labeled a "radical feminist" by some of the women at the retreat and criticized for not showing proper respect to the co-leader.

Relating the incident to my adult children, they hooted at the "radical feminist" label. "They don't know you, do they?" they asked, as I served them homemade peach cobbler. My children think I am a *very* traditional woman.

Even now, writing about that incident, I feel residual anxiety about "not making nice" about it. However, as embarrassing as that event was for me, it was a pivotal experience in my journey of finding my own authentic voice, facing the shame I needed to get over, and gaining the strength to speak about just exactly how the Living Christ had changed my life!

As I verbalized my experience and the memories of my public shaming to my directee, the feelings came rushing back to me, demanding to be felt and interpreted through my new lens of understanding.

Later, driving home from that conversation, I examined my strong reaction, recognizing that what my directee had experienced had touched something deep within my own life. She had activated a memory, actually, and I needed to revisit the various ways I pick up others' feelings and carry those feelings for them. When it is guilt or shame that I "catch" from other people, I deprive them of the opportunity of facing it themselves.

Sitting at a red light and pondering the issue of shame, the Kansas City resolution came roaring up from the basement of my memory. I was stunned at the realization that I have carried shame about even *wanting* to do what women in my world are not supposed to do. *When I remembered the resolution in Kansas City, I felt a sickness in my soul.*

That wound, inflicted to my soul in Kansas City more than two decades before, came boiling up to the surface of my conscious mind, demanding to be recognized, named, and healed. Finally, I had the ego strength to face what I couldn't face in Kansas City and allow the grace of God to tend that wound.

In that moment, as well, it was as if I felt a connection with all women who carry shame, and I sensed a new facet of my calling beginning to form in my mind. Indeed, we all carry shame, but it is the shame women carry that I most easily understand.

I've often said, jokingly, that one of the reasons we have the Garden of Eden story is so that we could know that from the beginning and from that time forward, women have been carrying Eve's shame in one form or another. It never hit me quite so hard, though, until that moment at the red light at the intersection of Alabama and Buffalo Speedway.

That thought might be considered ludicrous if it hadn't been expressed in the Kansas City resolution, made by the very religious group, my spiritual family, in which my spirituality and my sense of worth as a woman had been formed.

I had said to my directee, "I'm not sure if this belongs to me or to you," owning the fact that I had a strong response to her situation. Later, I knew for sure that I was clear about what belonged to her and what belonged to me, and what was now my responsibility was to unpack something in my own memory, bring it out in the open, and let the fresh breezes of the Holy Spirit blow over it in a new way. I was also clear that my primary shame concerned breaking the rules about what was acceptable for a woman to be and do in my religious culture. I had shattered stereotypes, and now it was time for me to deal with the shame I carried about doing that. For goodness' sake, I felt ashamed about following the calling that God had given me; I felt a need to hide my light under a bushel!

What lies beneath our defense mechanisms and our masks—our fig leaves—are layers of shame and guilt, often outside our conscious awareness but doing their damage at an unseen level, nevertheless.

What lies beneath our personas are the lies that hide the light of the True Self.

Indeed, what lies we tell ourselves and each other to go along and get along!

That clarity and breakthrough of grace was part of a series of events and synchronicities that began on a Sunday morning almost a year before.

Right after I signed a contract for this book, my friend Chris Drake came up to me after church and asked if I had seen an op-ed piece in the *Houston Chronicle* in which a professor named Brené Brown explored the outrage against the Dixie Chicks over their comments about the war in Iraq and the price women pay for keeping silent and "making nice." "You're going to want to read this for research for your book," Chris told me.

As soon as I found the piece, I decided that not only did I have to find Dr. Brown's book, but that I must meet her and talk with her. The next night, I was signing up for a class at the C. G. Jung Education Center, and there in the bookstore was her book! Within minutes of purchasing the book, two of my friends said to me, "You *have* to meet her!" Indeed, I met Brené Brown, and even better, she has become a friend.

Frankly, I'm embarrassed to admit how little I knew about the silencing of women in the church, but the truth is that it seemed almost *natural to me*, as if that was the way it was *supposed* to be! A lady, after all, doesn't impose her opinions on others, and she certainly doesn't if they conflict with the rules of the prevailing power structure.

Reading Brené's book on shame and listening to her lectures, I became more attuned to the way our culture cultivates shame in people through advertising and role expectations. It was Brené who shed bright lights on the ways marketing and advertising, cultural role expectations, and unspoken rules for men and women perpetuate shame. Referring to her own extensive research and experience, Brené stunned the audience by listing the standards by which women are judged.

Even in today's "enlightened" world, the top three attributes women are supposed to exhibit are *being nice, being thin, and taking care of others*, and when a woman doesn't meet those standards, she is often shamed and feels ashamed. We are also supposed to be modest. No wonder I have felt ashamed when I've been in the limelight!

Indeed, shame and guilt are two of the afflictive emotions that permeate and poison our daily transactions with each other. Even as I write these words on this cold winter day, I struggle with the feelings of guilt over not being able to help my adult daughters with their children today, a school holiday. This guilt is irrational, and I can talk myself out of it for a few minutes, but it is so highly reminiscent of my active years of mothering when I lived with the guilt I hear countless women express. If we stay home and care for our children, we feel guilty for not bringing in money and being productive, and if we leave our children and go out into the workplace to earn a living, we feel guilty for neglecting our children!

I cannot speak for men and guilt, but I do know that most women I know carry a lot of guilt, and underneath the crippling feeling that's all about what we have done that we shouldn't have done or what we didn't do that we should have done is the terrible demon of shame about who we are . . . or who we aren't.

Brené Brown also discusses that the cultural expectation is that men are supposed to win, exhibit emotional control, and take risks, and the absence of those attributes or behaviors is cause for shame for them.

Brené says that she is often asked why her research on shame is centered on women, and why her book is geared toward women. She responds first by saying that she is continuing her research with men, but also by saying that her publisher thought that women would be the ones buying the books. Perhaps women, carrying the burden of Eve, are most often the ones who feel both the pain of circumstances and the responsibility to do something to alleviate the suffering.

I do know that when a man begins to address the issues that are tearing his family, his company, his own life, and his world apart, what can happen is often miraculous. When a man can face his demons, everyone benefits.

Awareness, again, is the first step, and once I began to look at my personal issues about shame, that terrible feeling that Brené often says makes us feel small, diminished, disconnected, inadequate and never quite good enough, I knew the awareness would lead to a relinquishment, ultimately, and with that I would experience a freeing up of energy that could be used to connect with others.

Reading Brené's book and doing some deep inner work on the issue of shame, I worried through some more layers of denial about those feelings of not being good enough, thin enough, working hard enough, or keeping quiet enough. I began to recognize the ways that shame permeates our culture and how I had "caught" shame that didn't even belong to me. I learned how my world is complicit in keeping me feeling ashamed; when I play the role assigned to me by my religious culture, I don't rock the boat.

In our culture, there is resistance to being open and vulnerable, empathic and sensitive, all feminine qualities whether exhibited in a man or a woman. I also know that in our culture, we continue to be confused about how we feel, as people, about the expression of emotion. When a 300-pound athlete cries like a baby on the sidelines of a football field after losing a game or people go crazy with emotion in the stands at that same sporting event, it's acceptable, but when a man or a woman expresses vulnerability and, for goodness' sake, cries or chokes up, we deal with our collective discomfort by analyzing that moment to death, interpreting the emotion from our own perspective or explaining it away.

Men and women alike are scared to feel and scared to reveal those feelings, and so we put on fig leaves to hide our true feelings from each other. We construct elaborate defense mechanisms and masks to stay in charge, remain in control, and appear to be tough and strong and powerful.

Feelings, however, pushed underground will come out in some other way—in a physical symptom or condition, addictive behavior, depression, or some form of external crisis.

When we refuse to feel, we don't get to choose which feeling we suppress, and so we finally lose our capacity to feel love, joy, delight, and gladness. The longer we push down our feelings and the more we push away the truth of our feelings, the more that energy will emerge in violent ways, enacted upon ourselves or on others.

When I first began a process of spiritual direction with Bishop Michael Pfeifer in San Angelo, Texas, he made a wonderful, life-affirming comment about my spiritual life and my calling. What he said was positive and encouraging, and it didn't fit with my view of myself. It was, as I remember, a comment that had the capacity to help me see myself with more self-respect and to view my work with more gravity.

I remember being so uncomfortable with his view of me (and the call to a greater responsibility toward my work if I accepted his comment) that I deflected his words by relating the Southern Baptist Convention resolution about women. It had been seven years since I'd witnessed the passing of that resolution, and I don't recall having giving it ten minutes' worth of conscious thought in all those years, and yet, my first reaction to a call to responsibility and self-dignity was to drag it up out of the basement.

"But Bishop Mike," I said, "don't you know that a resolution was passed by the Southern Baptist Convention stating that women couldn't be in ministry because sin came into the world through a woman?"

Now I know that I was hiding behind the resolution, shrinking myself down to its size, and in doing so, protecting myself with a fig leaf of self-deprecation. It was as if I wanted to hide behind that resolution, partly out of a fear of growing up and being responsible and partly out of a fear of being condemned if I did.

Bishop Mike looked shocked. He sat there for a long, quiet minute, looking at me with a most grave expression, and then he said, "But, Jeanie, the Savior also came into the world through a woman."

Indeed, he did.

Amazing grace, mediated and spoken through human instruments, has the power to change lives. Speaking grace to each other, extending the power of God's liberating love, has the potential of joining us together for good. Grace heals the wounds of a lifetime.

Questions for Reflection and Discussion

1. Dr. Brené Brown posits shame and empathy on two ends of a continuum. Recall a time when you felt shame. How did that feeling of shame keep you from being able to have empathy for someone else?

2. You may not think you have any shame issues. When was the last time you were embarrassed about something? *How did you feel?* When was the last time you knew that you didn't want someone to find out about you or your family? *How did you feel?*

3. Have you ever shamed another person, either intentionally or inadvertently? What was that like for you? What was it like for the other person? How did you justify your behavior? Did you attempt to apologize for your behavior?

4. Can you think of any way that shaming someone else has a positive outcome? Explain.

5. In what ways does shame keep men and women distant from each other?

6. Does your religious group hold the view that women cannot be in ministry because sin came into the world through a woman? Is there possibly a difference between the public position of your group and the unconscious one? Explain.

Taking Action

Take a moral inventory of your own inner world. Identify the ways shame and guilt keep your separate from other people. Now that you know it, what will you do about it?

Women's Brains Do That, You Know

If Mary had been full of grace instead of reason, there would have been no room for the Christ child.

—Madeleine L'Engle

The more critical reason dominates, the more impoverished life becomes. Overvalued reason has this in common with political absolutism: under its dominion, the individual is pauperized.

—Carl Gustav Jung

Choose my instruction instead of silver, knowledge rather than choice gold, for wisdom is more precious than rubies, and nothing you desire can compare with her.

—Proverbs 8:10-11

In each of us two powers preside, one male, one female; and in the man's brain, the man predominates over the woman, and in the woman's brain, the woman predominates over the man. . . . If one is a man, still the woman part of the brain must have effect; and a woman also must have intercourse with the man in her. . . . It is when this fusion takes place that the mind is fully fertilized and uses all its faculties.

—Virginia Woolf

"You know what's wrong with that Martus Miley, don't you?" a man in the church my husband pastored asked another church member.

"It's that *wife* of his," the man continued. "That wife of his has read so many books she's blown a fuse on her brain. Women's brains do that, you know."

We could all laugh about this comment except for the fact that feelings and opinions about women's brains are still tainted by misunderstandings about the differences in men and women and the cultural prejudices that still flow beneath the collective consciousness of this "enlightened" age.

A highly successful female lawyer in a large and prestigious law firm recently sent me an e-mail with a cartoon showing five men and one woman seated at a conference table. "That's an excellent suggestion, Miss Triggs," the man at the head of the table says. "Perhaps one of the men would like to make it."

What is it, anyway, that makes a sound proposal more credible if it comes from a man? Is it a power issue, or is it a distrust of females and "the feminine"?

Only today I had an animated conversation with a woman about the issue of certainty. "I like a man who is certain," she admitted, "but when a woman is so certain, I don't like it." *What is that about? And does that say more about the speaker or the listener?*

I'll never forget the moment that conversation about women's brains and the problem I was to my husband was related to me. I remember the room I was in and how I felt when I heard it. The person on the other end of the phone was laughing, but I wasn't. He thought I would think it was as funny as he did, but I didn't. When I tell that story today, people laugh, and now, years later, I laugh. Sort of.

The man giving his assessment of my husband and me was supposed to be my "brother in Christ," but he was talking about me with an attitude I'd never encountered before.

At the time, I was young and full of hopes and dreams about life. I'd been brought up in a family that valued books and reading. Higher education and continuing education processes, clear thinking and the pursuit of wisdom were all important in my home. I thought it was my job to ask, seek, and knock on the doors of understanding and knowledge, and it had never occurred to me that my brain couldn't handle the rigors of learning!

In fact, I'd memorized 2 Timothy 2:15, "Study to show yourself approved under God . . ." when I was a very young girl, and I thought I was supposed to be a good steward of my mind.

Today I know that the man who made that statement said more about himself than he did about me, but at the time, what he said hurt my feelings. I'm not proud of that, and I'm not proud of the fact that it bothered me that no one came to my defense. Years later, I expressed those feelings, and it was suggested that what the man said didn't deserve a defense. I responded that while that might be true, I needed someone to speak up on my behalf. Looking back, I realize that I felt more insecure about breaking the stereotypical images of preacher's wife than others realized at the time.

With his statement, the man implied at least three things: (1) Something was inherently wrong with me. (2) Something is wrong with women in general. (3) What was wrong with me also infected and affected my husband.

What he announced about himself, however, was a prevailing belief left over from centuries of confusion, prejudice, and fear about women and women's ways of knowing. How often arrogance and ignorance prevail, especially when it comes to gender issues.

Whatever this man meant by what he said about women's brains, he was expressing an attitude that is dark and damaging not only to women but to men, but the damage done to women has been long-standing, pervasive, and perverse. I also know for sure that his disrespect and disdain for me, as a woman, and for women in general reflected a theology and an understanding of God that prevails in some degree in our culture and within the institution known as "church."

We are different as males and females, but as long as we focus on our differences and as long as prejudices and biases cloud our thinking about each other, we will stay separate and isolated from each other.

"More than 99 percent of male and female genetic coding is exactly the same," writes Louann Brizendine, in the *New York Times* bestseller, *The Female Brain*. "Out of the thirty thousand genes in the human genome, the less than one percent variation between the sexes is small. But that percentage difference influences every single cell in our bodies—from the nerves that register pleasure and pain to the neurons that transmit perception, thought, feelings, and emotions" ([New York: Broadway Books/Random House, 2006], 1).

Brains are different from person to person. The brains of men and women are different, and the brain of any one person is affected from day to day by hormones, diet, stress, exercise, illness, sleep patterns, and who knows what else. Women's brains do not, however, blow fuses when women read too much.

Perhaps the man who had a problem with my brain had been on the receiving end of the anger or frustration of a woman in a PMS funk, a mother who had been up all night for several nights with sick children, or a female who had been treated with disrespect because she was a woman. Perhaps he had felt overwhelmed by what seems to him to be illogical thinking on the part of a woman, or perhaps he had been manipulated by covert, hidden tactics often used by powerless women, but none of those experiences prove that women's brains are inherently inferior to men's.

Perhaps, too, this man had had to deal with "woman's intuition," that mysterious way of thinking that has always baffled and puzzled both men and women. Indeed, to a person who does not value it (or whose strengths are in logic, reason, and practicality), intuition, precognition, seemingly inexplicable leaps in consciousness can be terrifying.

Most likely, he was a person typical of our culture—suspicious of women and/or of right-brain thinking, intuitive leaps, and that which cannot be measured and graphed, counted and contained.

"Women used to be burned at the stake for that," someone said to me when I related an incident in which I'd had a premonition about something that indeed did happen, an occurrence that has happened to me many times throughout my lifetime.

Indeed, some women have been deprived of the opportunity to develop their thinking skills or gain an education that would have created more balance in their logical and rational thinking, but that women's brains can most certainly handle the rigors of higher education, complex theories, and critical thinking has been proven over and over. That women can learn complicated formulae, research in highly technical fields, and actually excel in areas that once were dominated by men is no longer debatable.

On January 8, 2008, the *Science Times* of the *New York Times* carried a review of the book *The Difference: How the Power of Diversity Creates Better Groups, Firms, Schools, and Societies* by Scott E. Page, a professor of complex systems, political science, and economics at the University of Michigan.

In the book, Page describes the importance of bringing different people with different ways of thinking into a process. People get stuck in their thinking, he says, and we all get stuck in different places. A different way of seeing the same things changes everything.

"When you only had men thinking about the economy," he said about the relatively recent involvement of women in the field of economics and in the work force, "they were ignoring the productivity of half the population. By including the perspective of females, the estimates got more accurate."

Interestingly enough, in that same edition of the *New York Times* was an op-ed piece exploring the difficulty we still have with the idea of women in power. The stereotypical female viper portrayed dramatically by Meryl Streep in the movie *The Devil Wears Prada* permeates our attitudes and blinds us to the reality that some women play fair, treat their employees fairly, and make excellent bosses. There are, indeed, cruel female bosses, and there are male tyrants in the workplace. Maybe there's something about female leaders that is connected to some of our unresolved feelings about our mothers, and maybe not.

Why is it that there is a prevailing fear or dislike of smart women in our culture? Why is there resistance to intellectual strength in a woman? Why are we so afraid of strong women, especially if those women are public figures? What makes us vilify a woman for having an emotional moment, and yet, if a man cries, we applaud him for revealing his tender side?

The tender place in me that my critic touched was not the part of me that "felt funny" about what he was calling "women's brains." At the time, I was still invested in believing in the superiority of rational, left-brain thinking over intuitive, right-brain thinking. A product of my culture, I overvalued logic, practicality, and that which can be measured, graphed, and put in columns and charts. At the time, I had not yet learned the importance and necessity of using both sides of the brain.

What bothers me now is that I was doubting, distrusting, and trying to disown my natural feminine thinking strengths, which are informed indeed by feeling, instinctual, and visceral responses and that mysterious process known as intuition. Thankfully, research about right-brain thinking has changed how we perceive the way brains work.

I wonder why it is that within the church this kind of attitude and talk is still allowed and is still so prevalent. Isn't the church supposed to be a place of respect for all persons and the nurturing of the hearts, minds, and souls of each individual?

Admittedly, Christianity grows from a tradition in which women were not allowed to learn to read and girls were not educated for millennia, but how long has it been since that part of our heritage has been laid to rest? Loving the Lord with mind, heart, and soul—one's whole self—is for both men and women.

Why is it, as well, that behavior that is no longer allowed in the secular world is allowed within the places that are supposed to be sacred? Why isn't the church leading the way in treating persons as persons, created in the very image of God?

Just what is it about "women's brains" that is the problem?

Indeed, both women and men are still struggling with societal changes, and women, in order to grow up and mature as human beings are designed to do, have made huge advances in loving God by developing both sides of their brains.

In breaking through the glass ceilings, correcting long-standing imbalances personally and collectively, and learning to set boundaries within personal relationships, women have developed left-brain thinking and masculine tendencies, and sometimes and in some women, that development has come at the cost of their instinctive feminine strengths.

All persons, men and women alike, think better when we can think with both sides of our brains, accessing feminine receptivity, openness, curiosity, and availability as well as masculine logic, clarity, precision, and decisiveness. Over and over, the issue is not about using one set of strengths to the exclusion of the others, but it is about movement and dynamism. Good thinking is about knowing when to use which strength and when to move over into the other side of the brain.

On the night before Hurricane Rita was supposed to hit Houston, our family walked outside to visit with neighbors who, like us, had chosen to stay home instead of making the now famous and nightmarish exodus away from the Gulf Coast. The sky was a strange color on that late afternoon, and as we talked, the wind became stronger. We exchanged names and phone numbers, and then each of us went inside our own houses, shut the doors, and prepared for the storm that never came. It was an uneasy time for us, but we also had a strange and inexplicable confidence that we would be safe and that we had made the right decision to remain in our home. Some people thought we were crazy to stay, and indeed, we took a huge risk.

Over the next few days and weeks, conversations in Houston revolved around who stayed in the city and why we stayed, and who left and what horrors those who left experienced in the long, hard drives to supposed safety.

My chiropractor, Dr. Gail Henry, an intelligent and highly trained scientist and physician, described the nightmare she and her elderly mother experienced, trying to go the short distance from Houston to College Station.

"Everything told me to stay in Houston," she said. "Internally I felt we would be fine, but I left because the two men in my life whom I highly respect convinced me to leave so as not to take any chances with our elderly mother. I did not want to be sorry I put my mother in harm's way, and so we left."

Gail described the terrible nineteen-hour ordeal in temperatures of more than 100 degrees with her mother who has diabetes and hypertension. "We would have been much safer here in my clinic," she said. "I would look over at her hot red face and feel awful for having her out on that road with nowhere to go but onward."

What was it, I asked her, that made her listen to those voices instead of her own deep, intuitive wisdom?

"It was because I respected the opinions of these two men and thought I should listen to their fear and pessimism when I should have listened to my own instinct! We would have been much safer here. I put my mother at much greater risk, putting her through that horrible experience, but at the time, it seemed logical to leave! I thought the men in my life knew best," she said, laughing. "I listened to their practical reasoning, when I should have listened to my intuition!"

Conventional wisdom seemed to indicate that the smart thing was to get out of Houston and head for safety in Dallas or San Antonio. It made logical sense to leave, and people who had lived through hurricanes made convincing arguments for leaving. There was no way to know for sure that we were making the right decision to stay, and another time, staying could be the wrong decision, but for our family at that time, staying was the right decision. But how did we know that at the time?

On a cold December night, I met my husband for dinner before he went back to the church for a night meeting. On the way to my car, an inner nudge said, "You don't have any business being out tonight," but I ignored it and decided to make one more stop for a Christmas present before I went home.

Getting out of my car at the shopping center, I walked along a well-lighted sidewalk and into a store with lots of other shoppers, and as I was walking in, that same warning voice told me I'd better be careful. I ignored the voice and told myself that I was being paranoid.

Leaving the store, the warning voice started again, and just as I stepped off the sidewalk and into the small space between my car and the one parked by it, two young men across the parking lot began charging toward me, moving rapidly into that small space between my car and the one beside it, talking loudly to distract me.

I turned quickly and rushed back into the closest store, and just as I stepped into the store, the manager asked, "Did they get you, too?"

Shaking, I asked, "What do you mean?"

"Were you charged by some adolescent boys in the parking lot?"

"Yes," I told him, trembling, wishing I'd listened to that warning voice and gone home.

The manager said, "Let me call the police, and I'll walk you to your car. This is the third time that's happened this week."

Later, reflecting on the experience, I realized that I didn't have any more respect for my woman's brain, that part of my brain that is connected to instinctual, intuitive, and mysterious wisdom, than the critic who thought I'd blown a fuse on my brain by reading too many books.

That night, sitting in the warmth of my house, wrapped in an afghan and drinking hot tea, I made a decision to start listening to my woman's brain and paying attention to the still, small nudges that come unbidden, asking to be honored and heard.

"I had a feeling that was going to happen," I've said to my husband and daughters countless times through the years when something I had intuited actually happened!

"Why don't you tell us these things when you have that feeling?" my husband has asked me over and over, and I have to say that there are four reasons that probably match my physician's male friends' reasons for leaving Houston.

In the first place, I have not always trusted my intuitive hunches. Learning to value and listen to those inner nudges has taken courage and practice. Sometimes, I still don't know whether those hunches are based on my feelings or a true inner wisdom or what we in my spiritual tradition would call the guidance of God's Spirit.

My daughter Julie and I were leaving St. Luke's Episcopal Hospital at the end of a long, scary day in which one specialist after another had been in and out, trying to determine the nature of my husband's illness. For a week, doctors had probed and prodded, trying to unlock the mystery of his symptoms, and over that week, we had heard them name frightening possibilities.

"What do you think?" I asked Julie as we walked out of the elevator. At the time, she was in her third year of residency at Baylor Med and knew enough to be alarmed about her dad's condition. Trained at two of the finest medical schools in the country, she also has had amazing intuitive knowing since childhood.

Finally, after a long silence, she leaned up against the wall and listed various possibilities, each of them scarier than the last, until I said, "Is that your fear talking or your intuition?"

Her eyes filled with tears as she pondered my question. "I'm not sure," she said, "I'm too close to this to know."

It takes consciousness and patience to be able to sift and sort through feelings, impressions, instinctual reactions, and thoughts to be able to differentiate between solid intuitive hunches and the debris of the mind! It takes years, I think, to be able to trust intuition, especially in a culture that values hard data, facts you can chart and graph, and logical, rational thought processes.

Most of all, it takes a kind of marriage of the inner masculine energies with the inner feminine ones to make sound thinking. I need my masculine strengths to give me focus when I've overused my feminine strengths and am foggy. I need clarity and order when I'm drifting in the confusion of too many ideas, too much information, and a profusion of options. By the same token, my masculine strengths need the influence of my curiosity and openness when I've become too rigidified or too stuck in facts. It's the dance of masculine and feminine, the cooperation of the right-brain and left-brain that create the best thinking, the most productivity, and the best communication with the men and women, boys and girls in my life.

Secondly, I have learned that some people are more open than others to listening to intuitive hunches, "the feel of things," gut instincts, and creative leaps in thought processes. We who lead with right-brain thinking, whether we are male or female, must be able to communicate our thought processes in ways that make sense to left-brain thinkers.

"You don't just go from A to B to C," my husband told me one time in utter exasperation. "You go from A to 17 to orange and then to R!"

Over the years, I've made an effort to learn how to communicate from both sides of my brain. I've learned to document my impressions with as much data as possible, recognizing that that which is perfectly clear in my head is sometimes a complete fog to someone else.

I've been cautious about voicing my intuitive leaps because I haven't wanted to join the ranks of those who pass themselves off as "psychics." There are people who interpret their intuitive hunches as "God talking" without taking time to "test the spirits." There are those who are not able to differentiate between their own desires, complexes, programming, and intuitive wisdom, and part of that lack of ability is the result of overvaluing the rational and provable and undervaluing or discounting altogether the mysterious, intuitive, and unprovable. It is important to me that my mysterious, intuitive, and creative leaps are grounded in reality and not just internal UFOs.

Finally, I've had to overcome fears of speaking up, especially in certain venues and with certain people. Perhaps I hold back on saying what I think because unconsciously I have felt the attitude of the man who thought I'd blown a fuse on my brain. Maybe I have held back because of the prevailing attitude in my religious world about the role of women. Maybe my insecurities are the result of "catching" that unspoken or spoken disdain for women and from the feeling shared by women everywhere of not being heard. And perhaps I've let the conversations and diatribes about "women in the church," leftover from Paul's culture, intimidate and silence me.

"Women in our culture are heard when they purr, whine, or scream," a therapist told me, speaking of the need for women to find their own authentic voices and to be heard with respect, listened to with openness and valued for their thinking. Scott Page, the economics professor, would argue that family, work, and government systems suffer when women's voices are silenced.

As women have excelled and progressed in the realms once reserved for men, having overused left-brain thinking in order to survive and thrive, they have sometimes neglected the other side of their brains. I see highly trained young women struggling under the challenges of raising children.

"What I learned in my MBA doesn't help me manage my children," a young mother told me. "How did my mother do this? How did she stay home with us and not lose her mind?" she asked.

"What works in my law firm works against me at home," another woman told me. "It's like I have to prepare myself when I'm driving home from the office. I have to picture myself taking off one hat and putting on another in order to be Mommy and Wife," she said, "and sometimes, it's too hard."

I am fascinated by the definition Carl Jung gave of neurosis. Instead of defining neurosis as a pathology that evokes shame, he said neurosis is an imbalance.

That one definition has not only freed me from some of my guilt and shame about my own quirks and defects, but it has invited me into the opportunity to discover and correct the imbalances that are revealed in physical symptoms, relational conflicts, work problems, and life struggles. If I can find where I am overusing one set of strengths and underusing another, instead of labeling myself "bad," "wrong," or "flawed," I can then, without judgment, look for solutions to the imbalance and put them in action.

That my critic operated from an archaic, prejudiced, and biased belief system about women, women's brains, and "what the problem is" is *his* problem, but the fact that our culture and, sadly, religious institutions allow, aid, and abet that belief system is a cultural neurosis that cripples both men and women and keeps all of us stuck in a quagmire of disease and dysfunction.

There are rays of hope as men and women in different professions begin to discover and implement "whole-brain thinking," valuing and joining feminine and masculine strengths in order to be more creative, effective, productive, helpful, and successful.

In the field of law, the letter of the law is an important principle, and we want our lawyers to be precise, correct, clear, and forthright. I deeply appreciate my lawyer's intense and scrupulous attention to detail when it comes to the business of my life.

However, there is another reality to the world of law and lawyers that, carried too far, creates a world where there must be a winner and a loser. Some lawyers are learning sophisticated skills in mediation, which requires the feminine strengths of cooperation and collaboration, openness and flexibility, listening and receiving. The goal in mediation is win/win instead of win/lose. Mediators work to find common ground and connecting links for the benefit of everyone, especially young children.

"I was beginning to hate myself," a mid-life lawyer told me, "and I was alarmed at the personal lives of my colleagues. Something happens to you when you have to make others wrong in order to be right. I had to go into mediation or die."

In medicine, alternative modalities, once held in suspect and disdain by Western trained doctors are now becoming part of the fabric of healthcare and wellness. The first alternative care physician I had who was trained in both Western medicine and Eastern methods of acupuncture, herbs, and supplements told me that the challenge is to know when to use which modality. Eastern medicine tends to work with the body, in a feminine style, and Western medicine tends to act aggressively to solve the problem, a masculine style. Both styles have value and are necessary.

In the business world, hierarchies are giving way to team approaches. In education, there are lectures, but experiential learning involves the student in the processes of learning.

My daughter Michelle is currently working in the Writing Center at the University of Houston and working on her PhD in English. When I give her a manuscript to edit, she ruthlessly wields her red pen over my words, cutting and sharpening my paragraphs so that they make better sense. She easily moves from using those masculine strengths to her feminine strengths as she interprets poetry and literature, those regions of the soul.

In the religious world and in the Christian church, long controlled by methods that look more like capitalism than the New Testament church, there are signs that suggest that the over-masculinized religious organizations are going to be forced to face the deepening spiritual hunger of human beings. It's no longer enough to give people outward forms, correct doctrine, and the rules; people are starving to death for an experience of the numinous, the Real, and the Mystery of God who cannot be contained in doctrine, rule, or ritual.

Perusing a table of books on the mind and brain at Barnes and Noble this week, I grabbed a new book by Daniel H. Pink, *A Whole New Mind*, which declares that right-brainers will rule the future. Of course, I bought the book, but I already know that while we will always need sound, logical thinking, it is good news for all of us when there is movement toward valuing the right side of the brain.

"How do you make your decisions?" I asked a successful entrepreneur, and he elaborated on his system of checking things out, making comparisons, doing analyses of risks, and gathering facts.

"After I've done all my fact-finding," he told me, "I trust my gut."

"Do you mean your feelings?" I asked.

"Nah," he said. "I trust my gut."

"Do you mean your intuition?" I probed, and he shrugged impatiently.

"That's a woman's way," he told me. "I told you that I trust my gut."

I took one more risk and pushed a little more.

"What's the difference between your gut and your intuition and your feelings?"

The man grinned sheepishly, and looked away. "If it's a man doing the thinking, it's in your gut," he said. "If it's a woman, it's intuition." And then he laughed and changed the subject.

My own father used to tease me about the number of questions I could ask about something, calling me nosy. "With women," he said, "it's curiosity and nosiness; with men, it's intelligent investigation!"

"How do you choose your clients and build this business?" I asked a friend of mine who is one of the top female executives in her organization.

"I follow my instincts and listen to my feelings and intuition," she told me, "and I let them lead me to the facts, the hard data, and the people I need."

We get where we need to go in a variety of ways, and we can get there better when we use masculine thinking and feminine thinking, and when we give equal value to both.

While I may teach and write about God, I do not speak for God. I don't believe in God as a glorified human being, but I believe that it must make God happy when any one of us becomes more fully human by accessing, developing, and expressing both sides of our capabilities.

Men and women alike have the capacity to move into the area of our lesser strengths and become more balanced and flexible. We have the capacity to move from half-brained thinking to whole-brain thinking, and with that capacity and choice come more freedom and greater possibilities.

Questions for Reflection and Discussion

1. Which do you trust more, your logical reasoning or your intuitive hunches?

2. What is it like for you when your fears inform your thought processes? your insecurities and feelings of shame and guilt? How do these afflictive feelings show up in your reasoning processes and decision-making? How do they affect your relationships?

3. What do you think it means to "test the spirits"? How does one do that?

4. Describe a time in which you didn't listen to your intuition. Were you afraid to know what you knew, to trust what you couldn't prove? What was the result?

5. Describe a time in which you did trust your intuition. What was that like?

6. Have you ever silenced someone else's intuitive thinking? What were your reasons for doing that? What was the outcome?

7. Have you ever beaten down a good idea, either your own or someone else's, by facts?

Taking Action

1. Ask a group of trusted friends this question: *How do you discern the difference between the guidance of the Holy Spirit and your own intuition? your own intuition and your fears? the guidance of God and your own will?*

2. Notice what bothers you about persons who think differently from you. Get to know them better. Learn from them.

The Mothers, My Mother, and Me

Help me to calm and quiet my soul,
like a child quieted at its
mother's breast;
like a child that is quieted, be so my soul.

—Psalm 131:2

We are all heroes. And the hero's journey begins at the moment of our birth. But the hero's journey for women is different. The enemies, obstacles, and battles women encounter are seldom as straightforward as those faced by men. They often exist within our own psyches and have been handed down to us by a culture that is only now becoming comfortable with feminine ways of being in the world.

—Christiane Northrup

"May it be done to me according to your will."

—Mary, the mother of Jesus

"You need the Blessed Mother," my spiritual director said in my first meeting with him. How could he have known that so quickly?

At one level, I was pretty sure that I could hear my father and grandfather, both Baptist ministers, trembling from the Other Side. Even now, I can remember my father's reaction to the statues of Mary in the cathedral in Santa Fe, New Mexico.

My dad's intense reaction to idol worship and the very idea of graven images should have scared me away from the whole idea of the Blessed Mother, but it didn't. In fact, I've had a holy curiosity about her for a lifetime!

At another level, I was clueless about what "needing the Blessed Mother" might involve. How would I get that need met? Who would guide me? And what might having the need met do for me?

At yet another, deeper level, I knew that what Bishop Mike was telling me was right, but the thought of entering into that journey scared me to death. All kinds of fears about the things I had heard about praying to Mary, adoring her, and "going to" her bubbled up to put me on edge. Other, deeper issues of rejection created some inner static as well, but I'd made a decision to enter a process of spiritual direction with this kind and wise man and I wanted to follow his guidance.

After speaking at a civic event for community leaders in San Angelo, Texas, I was seated by Bishop Michael Pfeifer, who had convened the event. As we got acquainted, I inquired about the process of spiritual direction, to his seeming surprise. My husband was the pastor of a Baptist church in San Angelo, and so it was natural that the bishop would be surprised at my inquiry.

I had been trying to find a spiritual director since I had first attended a retreat at the Church of the Savior in Washington, D.C. I had read a great deal about spiritual direction in which a person trained in this ancient process could help me discern the presence and action of the Holy Spirit in my life. Because of the ages of my children and my responsibilities at the time, I needed a spiritual director who was local so that I could meet with that person on a regular basis.

It took Bishop Mike one meeting with me to discern that I needed the Blessed Mother. I had no idea where that need would take me, but his initial, gentle suggestion was to set a path of asking, seeking, and knocking for me that I could never have imagined, a path of great joy and intense pain and suffering as the Divine Therapist began to heal the emotional programming of a lifetime.

Through the years, I have returned to that first conversation with a kind of wonder and a deepening appreciation for the sensitivity and discernment Bishop Mike had. Indeed, he did put his finger on the place where I most needed to be brought into balance and healed. Long years in a tradition that emphasizes the masculine side of God to the exclusion of the feminine side that is revealed in the Scriptures had put me out of balance.

"You don't ever need to read any more of the judgment verses of the Bible," a Bible teacher and psychologist had told me years before. "You need to read about the grace and the lovingkindness of God," he said. "You are too hard on yourself, much too hard."

I'd done some inner child work and a lot of journaling about the healing of the inner child earlier in my life under the guidance and teaching of Fr. Keith Hosey when I attended contemplative weeks at Laity Lodge. I had even led workshops and small groups on the topic, proving once again that we teach what we want to learn!

Within a year after that first meeting with Bishop Mike, my husband and I moved to Houston, and the first thing I did upon arriving was call the Cenacle Retreat House and ask for an application to enter their three-year Spiritual Direction Institute. It was there, under the gentle teaching, direction, and guidance of Sr. Mary Dennison that I continued to experience what Bishop Mike had told me I needed.

It took a lot of courage for me to ask Sister Mary to be my spiritual director, and when she agreed to do that, I knew that something important was going to happen to me. As I met with her time after time, I experienced in her gentle, loving, and patient presence something that I knew had to be like the presence of the Blessed Mother. She was receptive to me, open and available. She was tender, but strong when she needed to be. Under her gaze of acceptance and delight over the years, the little child in me began to relax and open up the places that had been walled off and sealed, places wounded from deep rejections by significant people in my life. It was with Sister Mary that I began to sense and know the feminine side of God.

As our class met week after week, my eyes were often drawn to a simple wooden carving of a mother gazing at her infant. Increasingly, I was drawn to visual images—sculptures, paintings, drawings—of the Madonna and Child or of mothers with their children. I didn't realize at the time how I was being led deeper and deeper into a journey that would connect me with my own feminine self.

One night at the end of my three-year training, I was participating in a supervision group, and after my presentation, it was suggested that I needed to do some more work on the healing of my inner child.

As a nerve I thought was buried deep was exposed, my reaction was instantaneous, defensive, and strong. I thought I'd dealt with that wounded inner child enough, and I *did not* want to deal with it again! Looking back, I recognize that I thought if I read about it, understood it intellectually, and could lead small groups about it, I had attended to it.

In the mysterious ways of the Spirit, I was led to the next phase of my journey on a warm fall day in 1998, when a friend called with an invitation.

"I think you'd like to take this course on Jung's Map of the Soul," my friend said, and with that invitation, I decided to join three other adult seekers and fifteen or so college students every Thursday afternoon for a beginner's course in Jung's theories.

From the early 1970s, when my husband and I were introduced to the writings of Paul Tournier, the Swiss psychiatrist who combined the disciplines of spirituality and psychology and had studied under Carl Jung, I had been interested in depth psychology. The writers who influenced my early adult life—Morton Kelsey, John Sanford, Elizabeth O'Connor, Keith Miller, and others—all referenced Carl Jung, and I had been interested in the process of Jungian analysis through their work and through my exposure to the Twelve Steps of Alcoholics Anonymous and our spiritual growth groups, designed by Cecil Osborne. Those groups, called Yokefellow spiritual growth groups, also were informed by the work of Carl Jung.

At the time I took this course at the University of Houston, my mother had just died, and of course that process was stirring up all kinds of feelings that I had long banished to the basement of my consciousness.

It was in the class on Jung's Map of the Soul that I learned crucial pieces of truth, and these truths would both form the foundation for the new process of growth that lay ahead and beam a light in the direction I needed to go in order to *experience* the healing of an old, old wound and the wonder of learning how to be my own mother. Sitting there in that classroom in the Honors College with pink-haired geniuses and tattooed students with nose rings and unbelievably bright minds, I learned about the three mothers we all have, and more.

As Pittman McGehee lectured each week, any mention of the mother/child relationship grabbed my attention. It was as if the information was spoken directly to me over a loud speaker, and I wanted to know more about the three mothers that are common to us all: the archetypal mother, the biological mother, or the mother complex.

"The need for the mother is archetypal," Pittman McGehee said. "That is to say, it is imprinted in each of us in equal amounts, irrespective of time of birth, place of birth, gender, or ethnic origin. It is the same for each of us. It is our first longing. It is of such magnitude that we will try to make a mother of anything." I was fascinated as he recalled the study of the monkeys who tried to make mothers out of wire monkeys wrapped in cloth.

I was mesmerized, listening to the ways in which human beings project this need for the mother onto the university (Alma Mater), corporations, and institutions, including the church (the Mother Church). "We even call the phone company Ma Bell."

We call the church "Mother," and speak of "a mother church," when in fact, as some have suggested, the contemporary church acts more like a legalistic father or a fussy old man. We want the church to take care of us. Contemporary people speak often about whether or not a church meets their needs, ignoring, forgetting, or perhaps being oblivious to the fact that the New Testament calls for a radical kind of maturity that is lived out in mutuality, respect, and reciprocity.

Perhaps, too, we sometimes ask friendships or marriage to be "the mother," and sometimes when we get married or when we go home at night, we expect each other to mother us. In a healthy adult relationship, nurturing happens, but not when one adult asks the other to play mommy or daddy.

"I cannot be your mother," my friend's husband told her. "I can be your husband. I can take care of you in the ways a husband can care for you, but I cannot be your mother."

"I'm *not* your mother," wives often say to their husbands. "Don't expect me to be your mother. I'm your *wife*!"

It was when I heard the words, "It is up to each of us to become mother to ourselves," that I knew I'd found my growing edge and learning task. Suddenly I recalled what Bishop Mike had said to me about needing the Blessed Mother.

Indeed, asking other human beings to do for us what we must do for ourselves keeps the relationship bound and constricted, at best; at its worst, those parental expectations, shoved onto other human beings, separate us from each other, thwarting the growth of both the individuals within the relationship and the relationship itself. Adults ultimately must *grow up*.

All of us, as well, have a biological mother who birthed us. It is this human being with whom we have our first relationship, and that relationship is so important because it shapes and affects all of our relationships.

"It is the job of the mother to bless the child for who she or he is, to delight in that child, and then to help the child separate from her in order to become herself, " Pittman McGehee said early in the course. "And it is the job of the father to bless the child for what he or she does and to help the child separate from the mother."

That simple, profound truth is the foundational principle upon which good parenting is built. Everything else that you need to know about parenting a child flows from that principle, and with that principle are other life-changing principles:

- A father can be a good mother, and a mother can be a good father.
- Sometimes, one parent is called upon to act as both mother and father to a child. It's not easy being both, but it can be done.
- One of the tasks of maturing and of individuation, or becoming one's own authentic self, is learning how to mother and father oneself so that you don't ask another human being to take on that role for you.
- A person's image of God is formed by his or her association with these earliest deities, the parents or caregivers. That image of God is formed unconsciously by the infant and is based on how the parents treat the child.
- Every child unconsciously begins life asking these questions:

Am I safe here? Am I wanted? Who is in charge? What do I have to do to get my needs met?

The reality is that none of us had a perfect mother, and most of us got too little nurturing or too much. Some of us got both too much or too little all in the same day, given what was happening with that young girl or young woman who birthed us, but however it was with her and whatever she was able to give, that primary relationship set us on our way. From her and with her, we formed our image of God and our image of ourselves, and it is from her that we had to separate at birth and in stages all through our lives.

It is the job of the mother to nurture us, first in her womb, and then it is her job to feed us and care for us physically. It is a good thing, a very good thing, when she can nurture us spiritually, emotionally, intellectually, and psychologically so that we have what we need to leave her and become separate, individuated, and autonomous. Some mothers, however, hold on too long. Some mothers push us out or away too soon, and all of that affects how we perceive God, how we feel about ourselves, and how we relate to the rest of the world.

My relationship with my biological mother shaped every decision I made and how I set up my life, though I did not know that until I began a process of depth analysis. The earliest programming worked for me for a long time until, as they say today, it didn't. It is true that the beliefs, behaviors, and habits that keep you alive for the first half of life may keep you from living in the second half of life.

Long before I understood anything about Jung's theories of depth psychology or read Alice Walker's *The Drama of the Gifted Child*, I had taken on the role of emotional caring of my own mother. My ability to block out my own needs and take care of her needs was so ingrained that it felt *right* to me.

I was determined, however, that when I had my own children, I would meet their emotional needs. I would be present to them and I would put them and their activities at the top of my priority list.

One day, I was driving my elderly parents from San Angelo to Odessa, Texas, so that my mother could visit her brother. As we drove through the barren landscape, my mother began telling a story about something her own mother had done. My grandmother, widowed in her thirties with eleven children, had had to put the youngest three in an orphanage for a period of time. My mother was one of those youngest children, and for years, she was too ashamed of that experience to talk about it, and when she was able to talk about it, it always made my father weep.

"By the time I came along," my mother said, "Mama didn't have anything to give. She didn't have anything because no one was giving her anything."

I remember gripping the steering wheel and taking deep breaths as she told about her experience. "Now I understand about her wound," I told my husband later. "Now I get it about her and about me," and from that time until the very moment she died, I worked harder to *be there for her*, by phone, by letters, by presence. For my entire life, I felt responsible for my mother's emotional state of being. Giving her happiness and keeping her from being sad was, I thought, my job.

What I was to discover was that not displeasing her and behaving so that she would not reject, abandon, or shun me had formed the primary relationship script of my life.

"You have a mother complex as big as the Astrodome," my analyst told me after only my first session. At the time, I didn't consciously have a clue what he meant and could never have imagined the journey that lay ahead of me. A part of me, the part that is wise and intuitive, knew. The part of me that yearned for wholeness knew and had led me to a place and a process, a container in which I would experience healing. Now I know that that declaration echoed what Bishop Mike and the Bible teacher/psychologist had said to me.

Of all the contributions to the understanding of the human psyche that Jung gave, it is the idea of the complexes that is perhaps the most profound. A complex is a complex of energy, actually, and as the writer and Jungian analyst Robert Johnson says, "We don't have a complex; it has us!" Indeed, being in a complex can feel as if some autonomous and willful force possesses you.

Complexes are like splinter personalities. They have core beliefs, a certain voice, a feeling tone, body responses, and particular behaviors. Indeed, it is complex theory that helped me understand even more deeply the importance of Jesus' asking the demoniac his name. Jesus evoked a deep understanding in the man of the various and competing forces warring within him. "My name is Legion," the man said. Indeed, all of us have "many" voices within us.

There are all kinds of complexes, but the parental complexes have an unusual force, it seems, because they are so primitive. When you are in a complex, you might say, "I just wasn't myself today," or "That wasn't like me," and others might say, "Who was it, then?"

The Negative Mother, *the complex,* says, "I will love you if you please me," and so the worth of the child—regardless of the age of that child!—is directly in proportion to the child's ability to please the parents. The Negative Mother has a shaming, withholding, passive-aggressive "personality." Shunning and pouting are two of her favorite ploys.

The other parental complex, the Negative Father, on the other hand, says, "If you break the rules, I'll punish you." The Negative Father is more punitive and exclusive. Operating *from within us,* he controls with fear.

It is the mother complex that has me in its grips when I fall into unconscious caretaking, forgetting my own needs and taking on responsibility that isn't mine, and it is the mother complex that sneaks up behind me to pinch me on the arm when I displease her. Sometimes, I have to speak rather firmly to *that* mother and put her in her place!

For many women, it is common to spend their lives meeting the needs of others and neglecting their own needs. Some of us, in fact, become "gifted" in shutting down our needs in order to take care of our parents. That is how good caretakers and codependents are formed!

In listening to young mothers describe the feelings of loneliness and isolation in parenting, I recall feeling overwhelmed at times by the daunting tasks of childcare. Often, young mothers are barely out of adolescence themselves and are transitioning from a job or career into the unrelenting demands of motherhood. Nearly always, mothers feel the pressure to live up to idealized and impossible images of "Mother."

In this society of competitiveness and the pressures to achieve and perform, mothers are often prone to comparing the achievements of their children. I am stunned at the entrance requirements for some preschools and the pressures parents feel to provide "the right" *everything* for their children. "Mothering is not a competitive sport," a wise mother told her daughter, a new mother herself.

Women report feeling the pressure to be "the Perfect Mother," and regardless of what that might entail for that particular woman, it includes the implicit message that she *should* instinctively know how to mother, whether she was mothered well or not, she *should* be able to subjugate all of her needs to the needs of her infant, she *should* meet all of her own needs, not get tired, and have an endless supply of love, affection, and patience whether she's had a good night's rest or not.

"Becoming a mother," my friend said, "is signing up for one long, continuous guilt trip."

My Vietnamese friend tells me that in her country, a young mother is cared for with deep respect and tenderness in the months after she has given birth. "We believe that if we take care of the mother, she will be healthier and her babies will thrive." In America, we pride ourselves on having our mothers back on the job as soon as they get home from the hospital and back at work as quickly as possible.

The power of the three mothers is huge. By reflecting on, analyzing, and understanding these three mothers and our need for the Mother, by seeing the biological mother as a human being, and by becoming our own person, separate and apart from that biological mother, our relationships and our lives become richer and more meaningful.

All of us know devouring mothers who won't let go and who suck the life from their children, and some mothers who can't let go when it is time for the children to grow up. Some mothers act as if it is the child's job to mother them, depriving the child of her rightful needs of being mothered.

There are mothers who parent as if their children were projects. Other mothers use their children to make them look good. In his book, *Creating a Life*, James Hollis says some children pick up the message that their job is to please their mother by compensating for her unhappy life ([Toronto: Inner City Books, 2001], 21). He asks, "How many children are likewise enlisted into the impossible, not to say unfair, project of making their parents feel good about themselves?"

There are mothers who abandon and neglect their children. Sometimes the abandonment is actual, but more often it is an emotional abandonment so that the mother is there in body, but not emotionally present. Being able to gestate and give birth to a baby does not necessarily mean that a woman is able to mother.

There are also mothers who are so busy that they go through the motions of good parenting, but are distracted by other things and never fully present to attend to what the child needs. Distractions can be difficulties such as working to pay the bills or trying to manage a difficult marriage, an illness, a needy parent, or a sick child, or the distractions can be a demanding career, an active volunteer or social life, or the pursuit of fun and pleasure, to the neglect of the child's needs.

Most mothers I know, however, work hard to be there for their children, to attend to their needs and to let them go, appropriately, when it is time. And most mothers I know worry about the 5 percent of things they did to hurt their children and forget the 95 percent of things they did to help and nurture their children to adulthood. Most mothers need to stop their guilt trips and allow themselves to live in grace and forgiveness.

Part of the job of individuating, or becoming one's true self, is separating all these mothers from each other. It's about growing up, and it's about becoming whole and healthy. It is quite a task.

Indeed, we often bring the past into a present relationship, unconsciously creating the patterns we had with our parents or the patterns we saw between them. We taint the present with the failures, disappointments, unmet needs, and idealized images of how things used to be when we project onto someone our *stuff* from the past. We often either try to make a friend, a pastor or priest, a therapist or spiritual director, or some other innocent party act like a mother to us, and depending on how our earliest patterns played out, we either want to get closer or push back.

Recently, I was deep into a conversation with a man whom I respect. We were having a lively and interesting exchange about something, but all of a sudden, it was as if a curtain went down between us. I began to feel a resistance to what I was saying, and in a few moments, I realized that with something I'd said, I'd hooked his mother complex. Even though he had been gone from home and on his own for several years, something I said or a way I looked or held my mouth or gestured evoked a feeling state in him that was about his mother and nothing about me. "I'm not your mother," I wanted to say, but couldn't. He would have felt humiliated and embarrassed if I had even hinted that he had mother issues.

Parented by a smothering, needy mother with poor boundaries, this man sees every woman as his mother instead of who she really is. Those of us—men and women—whose mothers "devoured" us with their needs, their ideas about what we were supposed to do and be, spend our lives in defense against anyone who trespasses in our soul's agenda or our daily calendar until we become conscious and choose to change.

We also project our idealized images of how we want a man or a woman to be onto him or her, infecting the present moment with future hopes of the perfect friendship, relationship, or partnership and often hoping that this person will be "the mother" for us. We fall in love with who we think the person is, and that "love" blinds us to who the person really is.

"You're not who I thought you were," a woman said to a man.

"I've never been who you thought I was," this highly evolved man said. "I've always been who I am, and that's who I'm going to be. You'll have to decide whether you want to be friends with me or the person you carry in your head."

Sometimes, as a spiritual director, I am aware of a person's fear of attachment or an over-attachment, and I often wonder if that person is projecting abandonment issues onto me, either fearing closeness or demanding more of it than I can give. *I understand that and know it because I've suffered those fears myself.*

"Tell me about your mother," I sometimes ask a directee, after I've gained her confidence and built trust.

If I know what kind of relationship a person has with her mother, I can better understand her image of God and her image of herself. If a person hasn't said anything about her parents after a few sessions, I wonder if the person has already worked through issues related to the parents and has come to what we call "a good place" with them, or if the silence on the subject reveals a still unexplored territory.

"You have become an adult," James Hollis once said in a class, "when you can turn around and look at your parents as separate from you and as adults. You are an adult when you stop blaming them for what they did or did not do and accept them for who they are, for good or for the ill."

I have decided that that acceptance of the parents as adults and assuming responsibility for one's own life must be what is meant by the Old Testament commandment to "honor your father and mother."

Perhaps when Jesus refused to go home with his mother and brothers and "be a good boy," conforming to her wishes, he was honoring her by separating from her, following his own path and living his own authentic life and calling.

There is an incredible freedom that comes when you can be a good parent to yourself, and good self-parenting and self-care requires accessing both the masculine and feminine strengths. When you can care for yourself, generate your own life, and even come to the place of delighting in yourself as a mother delights in her child, it is then that you can give love more freely and with fewer expectations, and that is called agape love—the love that *lets be.* It is when you no longer have to hook your emotional umbilical cord up to another human being, an institution, an activity, or a substance to extract life from a source outside yourself. Instead, you can generate life for yourself and give freely to another.

Erich Fromm, psychologist and author of *The Art of Loving*, speaks clearly when he says, "Immature loves says: I love because I need you. Mature love says: I need you because I love you." Growing up into mature love is the ongoing, relentless challenge of us all. It is also an invitation to abundant life. When you no longer are moved and shaken by the programming that says, "I need you," you can honestly say to another human being, "I love you."

Mature love can join with another human being without being enmeshed or entangled. Mature love can connect with someone else or an institution with good boundaries and without losing one's own center.

The need for "the mother" is so deeply written in us that we look for "her" unconsciously, and we do ourselves and others a favor when we honor that need, listen to it, and let it guide us to our own self-care. Under stress, we often regress and need the mother.

One of my most difficult and tender moments occurred when I was with my mother, alone, as she died. If anyone had told me that would occur, I would have said I could not bear it, and yet, as I was with her in that holy moment of death/birth, I knew I had been profoundly privileged to be with her in a sacred moment that I would treasure for my lifetime.

My mother was ninety-two when she died, as her own mother was, and in the last days of their lives, each of them called out for her mother. It is significant, I think, that at death, we return to "Mother Earth."

In the safe containers of spiritual direction and depth analysis with women and men, I have been re-parented in mysterious and life-altering ways. Those containers have been like wombs in which I could gather the strength and nurture I needed to mother myself into this second half of my life.

What I do know for sure is that the Spirit who hovered over the formless void at creation continues to hover over my own life to separate light from the darkness, the water of unconsciousness from the firm ground of consciousness, and in moving within the depths of my unconscious, the Spirit, acting as Divine Therapist, has indeed changed the emotional programming of a lifetime.

The process has been long and tedious, and always it has felt like the process of birth. It has been messy and painful, and sometimes I have felt as if I were the one being born, the one giving birth, and the midwife. What I know for sure is that in the process, I have learned how to care for myself as a nurturing mother would do.

In the process I have become acquainted with "the feminine," that which is out there in the world and that which is in me, connecting me to the world.

I have experienced the feminine side of God, and so I suppose this long journey continues to bring forth what Bishop Mike initiated by his suggestion of my need for "the Blessed Mother." He knew what he was talking about, and I've learned that so does She. He knew how much I needed "the feminine" to become more balanced, and so does She.

She Who Is continues to give me what I need and invite me out into the wider spaces of freedom and delight.

Looking back, I can see that there was a Spirit directing all of these events over the years, guiding me to the persons who could give me help and hope and nurturing me to the processes I needed in order to "find the Blessed Mother," the Great Mother, the Mother within.

Questions for Reflection and Discussion

1. Are you a good mother to yourself? How do you repeat the same patterns of behavior and conversation with others that you had with your mother? How do you expect others to do for you what a good mother would do? How does that affect that relationship? How do you soothe yourself?

2. Is there anything that is unresolved between you and your biological mother? Are you able to see her as a person or do you see her only as a role? Are you satisfied with the adult relationship you have with your mother? If not, what is your part in that? What is not your part?

3. It has been said that children blame and adults take responsibility. Are you still blaming your mother? How is that working for you? What do you need to do to take adult responsibility in the relationship?

Taking Action

1. If you have a "mother wound," work it out or talk it out so that you don't take it out or project it out onto others. Tell the truth to yourself. Own your part of the problem. Forgive. Make amends.

2. List the gifts your mother gave you. Identify the ways in which she blessed you for who you are. Make sure you thank her, if she is alive. If not, thank God for what she gave you.

3. Help a young mother. Compliment her for what she is doing well. Pay for a baby-sitter for her for time off. Buy her a gift certificate for a pedicure or a manicure.

4. Make a plan for mothering yourself well. Work your plan.

The Mother Who Matters

"As a mother comforts her child, so will I comfort you."
—Isaiah 66:13

"O Jerusalem, Jerusalem . . . how I have longed to gather your children together, as a hen gathers her chicks under her wings. . . ."
—Matthew 23:37

It takes very little imagination to envision God as male. This image has dominated the imaginations and self-concepts of men and women for centuries. Our imaginations have been held hostage by God the father. The "grandest of human imagination" will most certainly come up with a plurality of faces to inhabit the heavens, and with names that move us beyond the limitations of an exclusively male God.
—Patricia Lynn Reilly

"Ain't no way to read the bible and not think God white, she say. Then she sigh. When I found out God was white, and a man, I lost interest."
—Shug Avery in *The Color Purple* by Alice Walker

Does not wisdom call out?
Does not understanding raise her voice?
—Proverbs 8:1

"Is it worth it?"
we'd ask, riding into
town on the first day
of vacation, and a chorus
of "Yes!" would
drown any resistance, and
so we'd meet our friends
on the cold morning road
and form the Jeep caravan to
Paradise.

We'd take the paved road as far as we could,
and then the dirt roads and the
switchbacks, climbing higher and changing gears,
and the sun would rise over the peaks. The Big Sky
was so blue it would almost make you cry,
and the children would
giggle and fuss until we
climbed past treeline and slowed the Jeep
down to a walk over big rocks and
then boulders, and everyone was quiet, as if
being quiet helped the driver
navigate the rocks.

We'd climb so high we couldn't
climb any more, and then we'd
start the descent until we had to
park the Jeeps and strap on our backpacks
with our lunches and gear and step
sideways down the mountain. The little ones
cried but the man in charge said they couldn't
go if they cried and so they'd suck it
up and we'd hold their hands and creep
down down down the mountain until
we stopped, breathless at the first glimpse of her.

Descending slowly, as if approaching the Holy
of Holies, I always wanted to fall on my knees,
for the beauty of her, sitting there in the wilds,

as if she were
the Secret of the Mountains. I always thought
Her name was Heart Lake, but maybe it was
Hart. It didn't matter to me because getting to
her was always as good for my heart as it was
my lung and besides, like the hart, I'd longed
for her all year from the flatlands.

The fishermen couldn't wait, and the children screamed
with delight when they caught a trout, and I'd hear
them talking about whether the fish were big enough to
keep for supper, but once my children were settled, I would
go into an altered state and contemplate her. There she was,
cradled like the Hope Diamond,
resting quietly on the pristine breast of
one of the Queen Mothers, the peaks of earth that rise
up far above the ordinary plains of Mother Earth,
her waters crystal clear and
pure and clean and blue. There, in that quiet
container, those still waters were like a mirror, and
I dove deep into them to see more clearly.

I'd watch the clouds float
by on her, reflections rippled by a fish or a wisp of wind.
Gigantic trees ringed her like an emerald necklace, standing tall
around her and reflected in her, too, and I'd
rest my eyes in the deep green, eyes wearied by too much sun and desert.
I'd take deep, long
breaths of the pine and spruce perfume,
and I knew that it was here in this Still and Sacred
Wilderness that life was almost perfect and that love
was possible and God was in all things, but most especially
at Heart Lake And I'd try to embrace enough of that place—
its sights and sounds and smells—
to last for another year or . . . for the rest of my life, just
in case I wouldn't ever see Her again.
Beside her, I knew what the oneness of things
was all about, and I was connected to the oneness.

And we'd eat our sandwiches and the smallest children
got tired, and we always stayed too long, but nobody cared.
We'd pack up our blankets, gather our trash
and our gear and trudge
back up the steep mountain and lean on the Jeeps, our
lungs screaming and our legs shaking from the steepness
and then, we'd notice that the clouds were gathering, and so
we'd hurry and pile our stuff in the back of the Jeep and
push the children into the Jeep, covering them with their dad's
old red Springdale Bulldogs blanket. We'd hoped to beat
the afternoon rains or maybe we thought that just this
once, they'd pass us by, but
suddenly, the wind would whip July ice sideways
into the Jeeps and the children would cry, so the dads would
stop and put the doors on the Jeeps, zipping the plastic
windows around us and we'd start back down the narrow
roads.

How was it, I'd muse, that the earth could hold that water
so still, just letting it be?

and then the rain would get stronger and the wind
would blow harder, and we'd huddle and shake against
the cold, and the water ran furiously down the unmarked roads,
making new paths that would disappear in tomorrow's rain and
threatening our Jeep with its force. We would hold on
tight at the switchbacks, and hold our breaths when the
driver had to gear down, leaning at a precarious angle on the
narrow, rutted road, and
hoping we wouldn't slip or slide
or get stuck in the mud, 'way up there in the mountains.
And the rain
was fierce, as fierce as the lake was calm, and the sleet
was ruthless,
and by the time we wound around and back down through the
aspen forests again and again and again and came out on
the paved road once more, our lips were chapped and
our eyes were stinging and we were spent from the

onslaught of the elements, wrung out from a kind
of primitive battle with Nature, our own and the Mother.

"Was it worth it?" someone would ask, and we'd chorus together
our loud affirmation.

Yes, we would cry, and then

Amen . . . Indeed.
Amen . . . and Yes.

It was always worth it
It is worth it.

There are few things that connect me more to a sense of the Presence of God like Big Nature—mountains, deep forests, oceans, big sky, giant oak trees, fields of bluebonnets, birth, death—and when I connect with Nature, I feel connected to my own nature, my own humanity, and the Source of life itself. It is a holy experience, and it makes me feel whole.

I've spent a major part of my life inside church buildings. I know my particular form of the institution and organization of church well, and at times, I've experienced the warmth and nurture of the living organism, the Body of Christ on earth that is beyond definition, woven together with acts of love and experiences of the holy.

Often, it has been in nature and cooperating with nature, as in giving birth to my three daughters and nurturing and nourishing them, that I have experienced the feminine side of God, sometimes her majestic splendor, and sometimes her fury. It has been in nature that I've come to understand that God is not confined in one place, but is the ground of our being, the animating force of life, the One in whom we live and move and have our being. It's not that I believe that God *is* nature, but that God is the Source of all that is. It is in being in nature and with nature that my experience of God has been expanded beyond the walls of the church, the constraints of doctrine and dogma, the limitations of ritual and rules.

And it has been in nature and with nature and at odds with nature that I have come to know that "the feminine" contains a wildness, a disorderliness, and a chaotic side.

"Mother Nature's having a fit," my mother would say during a storm, and her words always made me laugh, but they also reminded me of the destructive, devouring side of nature. We love to rhapsodize about daffodils and sparrows, but are also terrified of tsunamis, hurricanes, and deformities of nature. We love the idea of the "maternal gaze of delight" as the adoring mother beams her unconditional love into the eyes of her newborn child, but we tremble at the idea of her expectations and the pinch of her disapproval or demands of us. We love the beauty of nature and natural beauty, but we also know the horrors of disease, devastation, and death.

Often, after a storm, there is a particularly beautiful day, and I recall how my mother would say, "Mother Nature is showing off today after her bad behavior yesterday." Indeed, the feminine energies can be nurturing and lifegiving and turbulent, wild, and unpredictable!

It was in the high country of Colorado that I first heard Frank Pool talk about ecology. Standing along the side of a narrow mountain road on one of our Jeep trips, he pointed out an area of that wilderness where miners had gouged out the earth with little regard for the long-term effects of their efforts on the soil and the grasses, the trees and the wildlife.

Frank Pool, engineer and oil man, World War II hero, family man, and gentleman—and a man's man—was the one who first introduced me to the ideas of caring for the earth, working with nature instead of violating her, having dominion over the earth instead of dominating it. For Frank Pool, caring for our natural resources is part of our obligation of stewardship!

Who could have imagined that an idea that seemed so logical and so *biblical* as caring for the earth, exercising our stewardship over her gifts, could possibly become a political issue?

How we treat the earth, how we treat our own bodies, whether we respect our feelings and emotions, and how we care for our souls reflect how we see ourselves as people, made in the image of God. The neglect of any of those vital parts of life will come back to bite us.

The case for caring for Mother Nature and caring for our bodies is being made broadly and widely for those who have eyes to see and ears to hear, but the care of our souls and paying attention to our feelings often goes neglected. Heart and soul issues can always be put off until tomorrow!

In leading workshops on spiritual formation, I often differentiate between spirituality and religion. I define spirituality as our life with God who dwells within us. We are spiritual beings housed in physical bodies.

We cannot *not* be spiritual. We cannot *not* have a god. It was Carl Jung who said that it was not whether or not persons would have a god that bothered him, but which god!

Religion, as I see it, is how we live out our spiritual lives. It is what we do externally to realign ourselves with God and with our own souls. Religion is about external behavior; spirituality is about the kingdom within. Both are important and both need the other for balance.

How we relate to any part of life reflects the image of God that we hold in our minds, often unconsciously. For most of us, the image of God is that of a father, a heavenly patriarch, a glorified male. The fact that this is an unbalanced view of God is often not only ignored, but, if expressed, it is maligned!

"It makes me so uncomfortable to hear people talk about God as *mother*," a young woman told me. "Just give me *Daddy*!"

"What are you trying to do, talking about the feminine side of God, rewrite the Bible?" a good friend asked, and I decided to change the subject. Never mind that there are feminine images of God throughout the Bible!

"If calling God 'father' was good enough for Jesus, it's good enough for me," a friend commented, and the discussion was over.

"What's your problem with God the Father?" a retreatant asked me after I'd dared to mention a reference to the feminine side of God. "Why isn't God the Father enough for you?"

To set the matter straight, I'm not an activist about this. I don't insist on inclusive language, which annoys my feminist friends but keeps the others happy. I find it awkward to have to do the him/her, he/she thing all the time, and I don't feel the need to force inclusive language on people who find it offensive. I've taken hits from both sides of the argument about the feminine and about women.

"You could help us," a retreat participant and avowed feminist said to me at the end of a retreat. "You could say things that could change things, but you are hiding behind old language."

I felt her sting, and I understood her criticism, but I could no more side with the militant feminists than I could side with submissive women. Either extreme leaves out too much and polarizes not only my own inner life, but other people.

Even as I recognize and name the abuses of patriarchy, even as I abhor what my denomination has done to women, and even as I speak up for the role of women in the church, I am constantly aware of the good men on whose shoulders I stand, the balanced men who are respectful, fair, and conscious. I've chosen my battles, sometimes out of fear and sometimes out of a desire to avoid losing the message I want to convey in the quicksand of controversial positions.

And yet . . . and yet.

There's something vital and life-giving about opening up to the feminine side of God, and for me, to fall into the heart of God through contemplative prayer was the very thing I needed to repair an old childhood wound and expand my understanding of God, myself, and the whole world. There is something crucial about opening up to the unconscious, to the dream world, to one's feelings, and to the Mystery that cannot be contained or controlled. There is something powerful and transforming and terrifying about yielding to that which is called "the feminine."

My journey into the feminine side of God began on the day Bishop Mike made his diagnosis, though I did not know it was beginning. His gentle counsel and wise words to me, "You need the Blessed Mother," beamed a light in the direction I would go and toward the persons I needed for that journey, and so I started down the path. At the time, I had no idea where I was going, but I was pushed from within and behind by my personal pain and my natural curiosity, and compelled from without by the Mystery.

The truth of his statement exposed some uncomfortable and ragged, growing edges in my life:

- I needed to expand my image of God to include the feminine side of God.
- I needed to get in touch with blocked feelings and emotions.
- I needed to become more spontaneous and less constrained by my roles.
- I needed to move out of my head and into my body.
- I needed a new and improved, caring and nurturing "Inner Mother."

At the time of Bishop Mike's diagnosis, I had begun to move more deeply into the practice and discipline of contemplative prayer, and with that practice, I would be called upon to access and use my feminine strengths of waiting and letting go, opening my mind and heart, receiving and gestating the experiences I had day by day. What I did not realize at the time was that contemplative praying does take you into the feminine side of God's nature. I had no idea that "the Mother" was waiting.

For me, my need of the Blessed Mother did not mean that I was going to give up God the Father. For many men and women, the image of father calls up feelings of hostility, anger, fear, or disdain. For those who have been abused or abandoned by an earthly father, it is sometimes hard to relate to God the Father. On the other hand, some people welcome moving beyond an attachment to an earthly, human father to the heavenly Father.

Always, when working on retreats or in workshops with the Prayer of Abandonment by Charles de Foucauld, which begins, "Father, I abandon myself into your hands," I talk about the fact that it may be necessary to use another name for God.

I'm learning that both men and women also reveal much about their attitudes toward their own mothers when it comes to expanding their God-image to include the feminine side of God.

I will forever be grateful to the women of River Oaks Baptist Church and the women of St. Luke's United Methodist Church who have been willing to explore and discover the women of the Bible in new ways, pushing back the old ways of seeing Sarah and Hagar, Ruth and Naomi, Mary the mother of Jesus, and Mary Magdalene. The women of the Bible have given us ways of talking about "the feminine," the need for the Mother, and the feminine side of God. Gradually, we are moving together toward a fuller image of who God is and how much we need a balanced image of God. Little by little, we are beginning to explore the ways in which "the feminine" is denigrated in our culture and the ways in which that denigration, disrespect, and disregard gets hung on women.

We do have to use language to speak of God. I get that. What I also now know is that a full image of God and an adequate God-image require moving beyond the one image of "Father" to include the feminine side of God. God is Father and God is Mother, but God is more than any one of us can describe, and I still operate with the belief that I would not believe in a God I could define!

The truth is that the Bible presents many images of God. Sometimes I need the Great Physician, and sometimes I need the Comforter. Sometimes I call upon the Creator, and at various times I need to focus on God as savior, hiding place, advocate, or redeemer. Now and then, I need God as Father, and sometimes I need an image of God that is nurturing, nourishing, gentle, and tender—like a Good Mother. Like the Blessed Mother.

In pre-dawn darkness, I move quietly down the hall toward the meditation room of the Benedictine monastery retreat center in Snowmass, Colorado, for the first "sit" of the day. I slip off my shoes, place them under a chair, open the tall wooden door lovingly made by Pat Johnson's husband, and find my way across the room to my corner. Over the years of attending the eleven-day retreats, I've gravitated to the same place in the room time after time.

I sit down on my meditation mat, draw my woolen blanket up over me, and adjust the pillow that supports my back. Over the next few minutes, I hear others enter the room and find their own places, and then someone closes the door and chimes the gong. Another person reads the Psalm for the hour and then we move into the deep, rich silence.

Breathing deeply, I focus on my prayer: "Lord Jesus Christ, Son of the Living God, have mercy on me." Soon, my prayer is simply "Jesus," and then, gradually, my breath becomes my prayer. My prayer is my "Yes" to God; it is my consent to the presence and action of God, and I return to it as I need to realign myself with my consent. The prayer word is not magic, and the practice of Centering Prayer is not magic. It is a way of making myself available to God.

At twenty-minute intervals, we stand and walk slowly and meditatively around the room, and toward the end of the hour, daylight begins to reveal Mount Sopris; sometimes the sun shines on her, and sometimes she is covered with clouds. Always, I look at her and am reminded of the feminine side of God.

I'll never forget the moment when Pat Johnson, the magnificent woman who was pivotal in building the retreat center at the Benedictine monastery in Snowmass, Colorado, was showing my friends and me the meditation hall on our first retreat. Standing before the tall windows, she pointed toward the mountains and told us how the Indians had thought the mountain range that overlooks the Roaring Fork Valley resembled a woman giving birth. How appropriate that was for my journey, then and now.

There, practicing Centering Prayer, intent not on achieving or accomplishing anything, we wait for whatever God might choose to give us. Those hours of meditation, some of them almost unbearably boring and some of them glorious, are overseen by Mt. Sopris, giving birth.

One year in May, Mt. Sopris was covered with snow when we first arrived for the eleven-day retreat. About midway through the retreat, we began to notice that each day, a little more snow had melted from her as spring returned. It seemed to me that an icy blanket was falling off, bit by bit, and that uncovering came to symbolize the thawing out of my own inner life and a melting away of my defenses. Perhaps what was thawing, as well, was "the feminine."

Just as I've lived much in church buildings, I've lived a lot of my life in my head—thinking, analyzing, judging, planning, critiquing. Partly as a defense to the force of my feelings, I'd learned to analyze them so I would not be overwhelmed by them. As I felt safer with the feminine side of God, I began to experience a thawing of my emotions.

In spiritual direction, women express the discomfort they have as they have become more cut off from their feelings, and with that, their spontaneity and warmth. Paul Tournier wrote in his book *The Gift of Feeling* that one of the great gifts women have to give to the world is, in fact, the gift of feeling ([Atlanta: John Knox Press, 1981], 23). "Such is our modern Western world, advanced, powerful, efficient, but cold, hard and tedious; a world in which diseases accessible to objective study are vanquished, but in which neuroses related to lack of love are multiplied; in which we have amassed a great wealth of things, while the quality of life has deteriorated. The quality of life belongs to a different order, that of feeling."

For men and now more and more for women, emotional cut-off, blocking of feelings, ignoring of instinctual energies, and a lockdown in mental reasoning is a guarantee of trouble at some point. Men collude in a conspiracy of silence whose aim is to suppress their emotional truth, according to James Hollis in his book on male psychology, *Under Saturn's Shadow: The Wounding and Healing of Men.* "For men to stop lying, to stop participating in the conspiracy of silence, they must risk showing their pain," he says ([Toronto: Inner City Books, 1994], 105).

Eventually, Mother Nature exacts her price for the disdain of one of her powerful gifts, the gift of feeling, in both men and women. Reconnecting with the rich world of feeling can be the bridge of reconnection with the inner feminine and the outer man or woman.

I began opening up to the unconscious by paying attention to dreams and images that began to emerge in my mind, unbidden. Over time, I have learned to pay attention to those images that come to me, asking them to show me their meaning. Often, those spontaneous dream images and waking images reveal things about my inner life that are at odds with my ego position or comfort zone.

I began paying attention to my own nature, my body and its symptoms. I began valuing sensations that were instinctual, sensations that could give me information about the outer world and my own inner guidance mechanism.

"The feminine energies are like any woman," I was told. "Pay attention to them, and they will pay attention to you. If you don't, they may act up like any woman scorned!" When the feminine is silenced in men or women, she will speak in symptoms, diseases, relationship problems, depression, addictions, and other self-defeating behaviors.

The more I listened to what was coming to me from within, the more I understood a Scripture that had once been used by a Sunday school teacher to whip us all into line about our daily Bible readings. Now, with an understanding of the ways of the soul, I had to smile at how much that teacher had missed the inner meaning.

"Come near to God, and he will come near to you," recorded in James 4:8, took on new meaning to me. Reading the mystics, I began to understand at even deeper levels what Jesus meant when he prayed, "May they [my followers] be one with you even as we are one" (John 17:11).

In paying attention to my inner world, I was honoring who I am, and in doing that I was being a good mother to myself, a mother who blesses her child for who she is. In honoring that kingdom within, I was reconnecting with the Source of life and the center of my own life.

Over time, I began reconstructing my inner image of "the feminine," and that process involved forming an image of a portable mother who would be nurturing and life-giving to me.

My God-image expanded to include nurturing, "gentling" feminine strengths, and my valuing of my own feminine strengths has steadily increased. I've come to the conviction that caring for my body, mind, and soul is an act of compassion, and that I cannot really care for others if I do not care for myself. While that seems simple and easy, it has been one of life's hardest lessons for me.

The truth that keeps returning to me is that whatever I believe and feel about God will shape how I believe and feel about myself. Because I am made in the image of God who is complete and contains both masculine and feminine, I need to recognize, celebrate, and express both sides of my nature as well.

In the human Jesus, I believe we see the most perfectly balanced and, to use psychological terms, the most fully actualized and individuated person who has ever lived. We see in Jesus both masculine traits and feminine ones, and part of his power was that he knew when and how and in what measure to use which strength. He was male, but he was fully human because he could access both masculine and feminine energies, and it seems to me that to become like him means at least three things:

- Each of us is to become fully who we are designed and intended to be.
- Each of us is to join the masculine and feminine forces that are within us.
- Each of us is to connect with others in love. We are meant to love one another!

Getting acquainted with the feminine side of God has also introduced me to my feminine nature that is greater than any of the stereotypical female roles I play. It has forced me to face the ways in which both the feminine strengths and women have been misunderstood and silenced, oppressed and violated, all of which, I believe, comes from a distorted understanding of God, the damaging effects of patriarchy on men and women, and the fear of "the feminine." I have come to a new understanding that how we talk about God will affect how we talk about women.

Elizabeth A. Johnson writes in *She Who Is*,

> Patriarchal God symbolism functions to legitimate and reinforce patriarchal social structures in family, society, and church. Language about the father in heaven who rules over the world justifies and even necessitates an order whereby the male religious leader rules over his flock, the civil ruler has domination over his subjects, the husband exercises headship over his wife. ([New York: Crossroads Publishing Co., 1995], 36)

As I have learned more about the feminine side of God, the role of women in the church, and the ways in which misogyny still operates within the world, I've become more willing to speak out and speak up, but still, it is hard. If it were not so important, I could not do it.

Recently, I was asked to write a column for the November 2007 edition of *Vocare*, the publication of Baptist Women in Ministry. Gladly, I wrote the following column, "Mary Magdalene: Symbol of Redemption/Model of New Life."

Sitting in a women's group and discussing Mary T. Malone's volumes, *Women and Christianity*, I was thrilled and inspired by the impact and contribution of women to church history since its earliest days.

I was also thunderstruck by the ways women have been silenced throughout church history, often labeled and marginalized, held back, discouraged, and sometimes martyred for speaking up or speaking out or using their God-given gifts in nontraditional ways or in ways that challenged the status quo of whatever form of church they were in. Only recently, when I attempted to glean written words of wisdom from some of the older women in our church, I was stunned to encounter a profound and pervasive hesitancy to see and acknowledge their long-standing and important influence and contribution to our community of faith.

That Mary Magdalene wasn't really a prostitute, but had been stuck with that label for centuries didn't really shock me at first, but over time, as I began to realize the *implications* of that terrible injustice to her and to women in church history, I was rocked to my core.

It is that people throughout church history have accepted and perpetuated *the label* of prostitute for the Magdalene, creating systems of belief and practice to keep the lie alive that gets to me. That churches and denominations have been organized around *any* misbelief and mistreatment about the role of women in the church makes me weep.

And it is that labeling others within the Body of Christ is such a convenient and easy way to deal with that which is different or troublesome, challenging, or destabilizing to the status quo that really causes me to stop in my tracks and take stock of the ways in which I collude with labeling. That I have learned to label myself and others within the Body of Christ stands both as a screaming insult to the witness of powerful, devout, and devoted women throughout church history and a call to repentance for the ways I have disowned vital parts of my own life and that of my sisters in Christ.

The truth is that it is absurdly easy for me to label and disown parts of my life that don't fit with the outer structures in which I worship and attempt to have community. It frightens me to consider how unconsciously I can discount my opinions if they don't conform to the group opinion. I am stunned to consider how I collude with oppressive systems by silencing my feelings, disregarding my own wisdom and what I know to be true and right and good just because I've labeled myself or I've bought into the label of the collective consciousness of the moment.

The new reality in which I live and live out my own calling includes the commitment to a reclaiming of the original blessing given to both male and female at creation and a reclaiming of the parts of myself and other women that have been oppressed by prejudice and bias.

Scripture states that Jesus healed and transformed Mary Magdalene, and then he liberated her and empowered her, and my leap of faith is that the Living Christ is at work in the lives of all of us to do the same kind of work in us that he did for her.

Sometimes, I, too, don't know how to love Jesus, but I'm guessing that we love him best when we participate with him in loving each other into wholeness, and sometimes that requires radical courage, uncommon grace, and amazing patience.

It really doesn't have to take 1,378 years to redeem a woman today, does it? [Used with permission of Baptist Women in Ministry, 3001 Mercer University Drive, Atlanta, Georgia, 30341]

Just as Mary Magdalene has been redeemed, so, too can be "the feminine."

Questions for Reflection and Discussion

1. Describe your reactions to the idea of the feminine side of God.

2. Have you experienced the feminine, nurturing side of God? What was that like? Who has modeled for you the feminine side of God?

3. In what ways do you see the contemporary church enslaved to a masculine model and in imbalance? What does it do to the Body of Christ to exist under the "compete and defeat" rules of our culture?

4. What benefits can you see for individuals in nurturing a God-image that allows for the feminine side of God? How would a more balanced image of God benefit the church?

5. Why do you think there are such strong reactions against the notion of God's feminine side? What fears drive such reactions?

Taking Action

1. Find a person who has a relationship with "the Blessed Mother." Ask that person to explain to you what that means.

2. Take a child on an outing. Notice his/her reactions to the world around him/her. Notice your feelings toward that child. What do your feelings toward that child tell you about the relationship between your own inner child and your adult self?

3. It has been said that we get our theology more from the music we sing than from the sermons. Listen to the music in your worship setting. What image of God does it portray? Is it a balanced image?

Portable Parents

"Who is my mother?"

—Jesus of Nazareth

"If you really want to know someone, look at that person in the context of three generations. Look either at the generation before or after the person, or look at the two generations before or after him, and you will have a better understanding of who he is."

—Howard Hovde

"Honor your father and your mother, that you may live long in the land that the Lord your God is giving you."

—Exodus 20:12

Soulwork is the prerequisite, not only of healing but also of maturation.

—James Hollis

"I did not come to bring peace, but a sword. For I have come to turn a man against his father, a daughter against her mother, a daughter-in-law against her mother-in-law, a man's enemies will be the members of his own household."

—Matthew 10:35-36

In her first year of pediatric residency, my daughter Julie took an urgent call in the middle of the night to go to the hospital room of an adolescent girl. Not knowing what to expect, Julie braced herself, walked into the room, and quickly diagnosed one of the problems. The girl and her mother were having a loud and angry argument!

Julie describes asking the mother to leave and then sitting down beside the girl's bed, waiting for her to stop crying. Finally, the girl began pouring out her anger toward her mother, pausing between accusations and outrage to sob hysterically. Finally, she had vented her anger and became somewhat quiet.

"I've been this angry at my mother," Julie told her gently, and of course the girl was shocked to hear that, but Julie's empathy and identification with the girl's anger calmed her and normalized her feelings. The truth was that the girl was sick and afraid, and her mother was afraid, and as it is so often when we are afraid, we lash out at the person closest to us. Often, it is the mother who takes the hit; my wise friend says that that is because the child is pretty sure the mother isn't going to leave, no matter what.

What is it, anyway, with mothers and daughters and mothers and sons?

Why is it that so many people have "a problem" or "a mother problem" with the person who birthed them or raised them? What is it about the *mother* that causes us problems? What is it about the mother/child relationship that makes daughters roll their eyes and sons refuse to take the phone calls when their mothers call?

Is it that mothers are such a problem universally, or is it that we the children lay expectations and hang projections on them that burden them unnecessarily with our own childish agendas? Or is it a little bit of both?

I think that mothers get the worse rap until I hear the story of a son or daughter whose father abandoned or abused his children. Fathers wound and injure their children. Fathers abandon their children; they require too much of them, overpower them, and sometimes abuse them. We hurt each other because we are human and we are imperfect.

Often, when listening to adult children who continue to excoriate their parents, I sometimes wonder what the parents' perspective might be. Just as adult children may wish they had different parents, perhaps some parents wish they had had different children. Being unwanted *as you are* is a tough way to live—for both the parent and the child.

I have seen parents attempt to support and reach out to a child who rebuffs the connection. I have also seen parents who give generously or lavishly to a child, only to have more demanded of them. In the complicated world of parent-child relationships, it is heart-breaking when neither is who the other needs him or her to be—or when all that you do, either as a parent or as a child, is not enough.

We begin our lives separating from our biological mothers, and while we love to romanticize birth, the reality is that that first separation is laborious, painful, and bloody. The truth is that people sometimes die while being born, and sometimes mothers die while giving birth. Sometimes, separating from our earthly mothers is difficult; always, becoming aware of the parental complexes is complicated, messy, and hard.

From that first separation from the warm, wonderful womb in which we have to do nothing but exist and thrive, we must separate from our mothers in increasingly difficult increments for the rest of our earthly lives.

For sons, it is especially important that the separation from the mother takes place, and if it does not, that enmeshment will affect every relationship he has from then on. It is vital for a little boy to be "not like" her in order to become a man and to become his own person. This separation is so vital, in fact, that in some Native American Indian cultures, little boys are taken from their mothers at an early age and not allowed to look into their faces again. Indeed, without that separation from the mother, she is present always in the son's interactions with others.

I used to assume that the separation of daughters from the mother is not as difficult because there is not the expectation of being "not like" her, but my experience belies that. There's no point in comparing the difficulty, for every *person* lives under the divine imperative to become who she or he is. Daughters, like sons, must separate from the mother and become a separate individual, and they must separate from their fathers. There are few things more damaging in a marriage than a woman's inability to give up comparing her husband to her father, a sure sign she is stuck in the infantile position of "daddy's daughter." On the other hand, how many men, trying to give love and affection to a woman, have paid terrible dues for what a father did in her long-ago past?

Even the seeming "loving" or "perfect" parent to whom the child can do no wrong can set up that child, either a son or a daughter, for a lifetime of frustration with peers who expect the adult to grow up, reciprocate, assume the responsibilities, and bear the difficulties of a relationship of equals.

It's a fact of life that some parents are more of a problem to their adult children than others, but all of us carry around "the parental complexes," the inner mother and inner father that go with us wherever we go, pinching us on the back of the arm when we least expect it or making us act in ways that don't reveal the best of who we are. The phrase "If it's not one thing, it's the mother," may look pretty on a needlepoint pillow, and we may laugh . . . unless we're crying.

"I am forty-five years old," a friend told me, laughing. "I've been on my own for twenty-six years, but when my mother calls and asks me if I've been to church (or called my aunt, or remembered a birthday), it's as if I am back in her kitchen, showing her my report card."

In hearing the stories of parent/child relationships and in exploring my own, I come back over and over to the reality that sometimes parents are the problem, but it is usually those parental complexes, the portable mothers and fathers we carry around with us, that are the bigger problems. They are also the parents we must learn to "manage."

Thomas A. Harris introduced the reading public to Transactional Analysis and to the idea of the inner landscape that is populated with forces he designated as the inner parent, adult, and child, helping us to become aware when we operate out of one of those alternate "personalities." Harris helped adults and children alike become conscious of the free child, the reasonable adult, and the critical parent who acts as the Tormenter, the Judge, and Jury—all of whom reside within us. Harris gave us an accessible language to help us become more aware of the inner scripts by which we live, make our decisions, and enhance or cripple ourselves.

It was Jung's theory of the complexes in depth analysis that helped me understand how I could act as a mature adult until some provocation flipped an internal switch, when I would suddenly feel as though I were back in childhood, either fearing the punishment or rejection of a parent or striving to win the approval or affection of a parent.

How could it be, I wondered, that in the presence of certain people who reminded me of rejecting or punishing figures from my past, I could still feel like an unwanted child or that I was wrong or had done something wrong? Why was it that the same kind of person kept showing up in my life, evoking the same feelings I'd felt in childhood? Why did I keep repeating patterns that were not helpful or healthy?

Often, I would make a decision to do something that was good for me to do, only to sabotage myself by noon! What was in me, I wondered, that made me keep living out Paul's lament in Romans when he said, "The things I want to do, I do not do, and the very things I don't want to do, I do!"

In a complex, a person might say, "I just wasn't myself today" or "That wasn't like me," provoking others to respond with the challenge, "Then, who was it, if it wasn't you?" or "Yeah, it was you. Take a look at yourself!"

It was life changing for me to learn that without consciousness, we keep repeating the same patterns we had with our earliest caregivers. *Typically, it is the patterns we form with our parents that we keep repeating, and the place we most often do that is in relationships with persons of the opposite sex.*

Indeed, our complexes are formed when we are young, vulnerable, and needing to please or placate the persons who care for us. Sometimes, those inner parents keep us out of trouble or protect us, but at some point, we may need to fire them!

"My mother told me that I should always do that," I commented to a young friend as we boarded a plane, recalling some piece of advice that my mother always gave. (When there's an "always" or "never" attached to an inner message, it's a signal to look for the presence of a complex.)

"Yeah, well, some of the things our mothers told us we don't need anymore," he said, and I laughed.

He's right, I told myself, *and it's time I learned to hear my own voice as the authority.* I was, at the time, in my fifties!

A friend told me about growing up in Washington, D.C., watching his father debate with, as he said, "the best of them" in the Congress. "He was brilliant, articulate, and powerful in the halls of Congress, but when he got home," my friend said, "he completely wilted in front of my mother."

What was that about? Was the man's wife that overbearing, or did he go into a mother complex when he was with her?

How often it is that when there is a problem in a present relationship, the root goes back to a problem or a pattern from childhood. It is as if the original problem or trauma in childhood has tentacles that stretch out into the future, constricting and constraining a man or a woman when he or she attempts to have an intimate and mature relationship with someone in the present. Sadly, the children are the victims, as well, of those tentacles.

Most parents, however, do a good enough job of raising their children. Parents, unless there is some illness, do not decide consciously to injure their children. Parents hurt children either out of ignorance or affliction and sometimes because their own unmet needs are so great they cannot meet those of their children. Many of us have experienced either too much parenting and feel overwhelmed by a parent and his/her needs, demands, or problems—or too little parenting and experience the pain of abandonment or neglect. *That is life—our imperfect life.*

We can move around the world to get away from our biological parents, but the parental complexes go with us wherever we go. Our parents may have been deceased for decades, but they still carry the power through the parental complexes to control, inhibit, or defeat us. Sadly, we become so accustomed to the tyranny of the parental complexes that they "feel" normal to us, and yet, they rob of us our very lives!

James Hollis quotes the poet Shelley when he says that "habit is a great deadener." Indeed, our habitual behavior numbs us to the world around us and within us, keeping us asleep at the wheel of our lives, oblivious to the power and grandeur that is in us. Hollis goes on to talk about that which deadens us, "So is fear, and so is lethargy, the twin gremlins which sit at the foot of our bed each morning, each wishing to nibble away resolution and desire. They are the enemy, as well as the fact that permission to be who we are was so often conditionalized in childhood that most persons have to attain that existential freedom along the way on their own" ([Toronto: Inner City Books, 2001], 48).

I thought I was going to have a few sessions of analysis and be on my way, free and unfettered by the worries and problems that had brought me to the analyst's office on a warm spring day. When I began, I didn't have a clue where the process of depth analysis would lead me, but when the analyst said to me in the first session, "You have a mother complex as big as the Astrodome," I was more than a little stunned and disoriented. Maybe I was a little offended, too, and a little defensive, as if I'd been "found out," but I was also curious. Most of all, though, a part of myself—and I am convinced it was the True Self, the soul—resonated with the words and I knew that they were true. In those words, I could hear a calling to redemption.

Over time, I was to discover just how much the mother complex held me in a tight grip. I learned, as well, that every time I wanted to change, the father complex, sometimes speaking in a guilting feminine voice and sometimes in an authoritative masculine voice, would stop me. Unpacking those complexes, changing my mind about how I will live in the world, and learning how to live with more freedom and grace has not been easy. Analysis has been entering into a process of costly grace, and it has been worth the cost.

About midway through my process of depth analysis, I was forced into an uncomfortable decision. I say I was forced into that position because I have learned that the self often orchestrates outer events to help us break free and become conscious.

I was invited to an event that I believed I should attend, but the thought of going was creating an actual physical response. If the "should" component wasn't enough to indicate that I was in a complex, the physical response was! I knew that if did attend this event, I would be putting myself in a position of repeating the self-rejecting patterns of a lifetime. The parental voices hammered away like water torture, telling me I "should" go ahead and attend the event. Those voices were loud, insistent, and reinforced by all kinds of other voices that put pressure on me to stay in those same patterns. In fact, those inner voices were like those of a bully instead of a kind, nurturing, and protective parent.

I could tell I was in a complex because my angst about the decision was out of proportion to the importance of the actual event. I've learned that when my reaction to something is excessive, I'm likely in a complex, and when I am in a complex, I am not thinking clearly. When I am not thinking clearly, I will not make healthy decisions, and when I don't make healthy decisions, I keep getting the results I don't want.

Finally, I knew that it was time for me to take care of myself and stop my neurotic caretaking, caretaking that was designed to win, earn, wrest a blessing of approval I'd wanted all my life. Stopping that lifelong behavior would mean that I might displease people whose approval I wanted. It would mean that I would risk not being understood and that "they" would be giving their own interpretations to my action. Changing my behavior would also mean that I was taking charge of my life, getting out from under the bondage of the complex, and risking living my own life. Changing my behavior would mean that I would be a better mother to myself.

Reminding myself of the truism that we would worry less about what others think of us if we knew how seldom they do, I made the decision to do what was healthy, life-giving, and wise for the care of my own soul, and by doing that, I made one more step in becoming mother to my own life, and a good mother at that!

I've learned through intense analysis about how ego, the organ of consciousness, works and how necessary it is to have an ego. Ego is the part of me that gets me up and gets me around to my appointments and meetings. Ego keeps me behaving appropriately, but the truth is that ego is at the mercy of my complexes! The ego is made up of all kinds of adaptations to the outer world, and sometimes it wears masks. Thomas Keating calls the ego the false self, not as in untruthful, necessarily, but as in the self that behaves as the outer world expects it to behave.

The triumph of the Self, or the soul, is experienced as a defeat for the ego. I have learned that the Self is ruthless in accomplishing its purposes. In my case, the Self had been working hard to heal the wound of a lifetime, and the occasion that was presented to me—to attend or not attend this event—was about so much more than attendance. It was about my recovery from a lifetime of being controlled by the parental complexes that had me bound in a restrictive life. The True Self in me, God-in-me, was engineering a release from an inner prison of a lifetime.

All complexes act almost as separate personalities, and when we go into a complex, especially a parental complex, there is often a feeling of shame or guilt. The inner voices speak condemning words, often the same words, and often calling us names and saying things to us that we would never dare say to another human being.

The complexes keep us from living our lives. They keep us from being the spontaneous, free, and natural persons we are created to be. They rob us of our joy, and they either keep us stuck in the past or prevent us from living fully in the present moment. The complexes give us disempowering messages; they tell us either that we are wrong or that we did wrong, and often, that inner turmoil gets acted out, taken out, or projected out on other people.

Jesus said "the kingdom of God" is within, and I have learned that when the complexes rule my inner world, the kingdom of hell is also within, ruling over me with feelings of inadequacy, anger and hate, shame, guilt, and fear. I've learned, as well, that some people spend their entire lives living under the domination of those inner complexes, never daring to come out of that prison and live in the wider spaces of freedom and grace.

Being in a complex keeps me from living in the present moment; it keeps me chained to the past, imprisoned by worn-out patterns.

Complexes suck the joy out of the moment.

Being in a complex keeps other people from knowing who I really am.

I say things when I'm in a complex that a part of me means to say; the problem is that it's not the best part of me that is speaking!

Complexes prevent me from living my own authentic life.

Complexes keep me intimidated and fearful; they shrivel my life and deplete my energy.

Complexes make me feel normal; acting outside their control makes me feel uncomfortable at first.

We can inherit complexes from our family members, repeating behavior that we absorbed unconsciously.

In Thomas Harris's language, sometimes people relate to each other as Critical Parent to Critical Parent. In Jung's language, sometimes people relate complex to complex. Then, we wonder why relationships go sour!

In a complex, I give *need love*, loving because I need the other person or the other person needs me, or I love out of guilt or responsibility. Loving from my own authentic Self, I love freely, and the love is a gift.

When we as adults can differentiate between the outer persons who are our biological parents and the complexes we carry around with us, we have a chance of making peace within our inner landscape. Making peace within leads to making peace without. To grow up and form meaningful and healthy mature relationships as adults and with people of all ages, it *is* necessary to leave father and mother.

Jesus' strong and terrible words about severing our familial connections seem harsh and scary to us. I am convinced, however, that it is the task of each of us to do just that, and in a very real sense, *we honor our parents by growing up, separating from them, becoming responsible for our own lives, and then loving them as persons.* The extent to which a person can differentiate himself or herself from the complexes within is the extent to which he or she can form healthy relationships with other human beings, including the biological parents.

When two persons meet, each brings an entire committee from the past with him or her, and each of those voices has an agenda and a pattern of behavior. None of us encounters the other alone, and what is within each person either helps us connect with others or keeps us separate.

Whatever you call the habitual and reflexive behaviors that keep you stuck in an old and childish pattern of relating to others, the reality is that those patterns keep us separated from ourselves in an ongoing inner turmoil and conflict. That inner conflict gets played out in our relationships with others, separating us from each other and preventing harmony, sabotaging intimacy and closeness, and either crippling or destroying relationships with friends, colleagues, and family members. My perspective tells me that those separations and fragmentations both reveal and feed a separation from God.

In the Old Testament, there is a daunting principle of family systems that reveals much insight and help for contemporary families. In Exodus and Jeremiah, God speaks to the children of Israel about the children being punished "to the third and fourth generation." In fact, what does not get worked out in one generation is often passed down to the next generation and the next, injuring innocents along the way, until someone in that family becomes conscious and says, "This stops here!"

James Hollis, in his book, *Creating a Life: The Necessity of Personal Myth*, says,

> Whatsoever is unaddressed by one generation is rolled into the next by way of example, admonition, or omission. These unconscious, clustered energies, called complexes by Jung, are conveyed by direct experience internalized, or by the transmission of unconscious motifs whose influence may only be seen, if at all, many years later, and often after great suffering." ([Toronto: Inner City Books, 2001], 12-13)

Sometimes, talking about sin makes people uncomfortable. We prefer to talk about character defects or mistakes. I understand that, having been brought up in a culture that emphasized sin over grace, judgment over love, and punishment over forgiveness. When I was growing up, I understood "sin" to be the behaviors that my particular culture had taught me were sins, and I'm embarrassed now to recall the things I called sin.

When I became an adult and began to think for myself and read more widely, I began working with the definition of sin as being "separation from God" or "missing the mark," and in our Yokefellow Spiritual Growth Groups, I learned that most of us focus on the symptoms, the things we do, instead of the real cause. The real cause of our behaviors that separate us from God and others and prevent us from living up to who we really are those inner demons of fear, guilt, and shame, feelings of inadequacy, hate, and anger, and the complexes love to employ those afflictive emotions to keep us disempowered and separated from others.

My wise West Texas friend Travis Perry used to say, "Jeanie, we are punished as much by our sins as for them!" Indeed, all of us reap the consequences of our choices, and sometimes others reap the consequences of our choices as well.

Complexes are going to sneak up on us from time to time, especially under stress or fatigue, but to live possessed by a complex is to live in bondage to forces that diminish and demean us.

In the Gospel of John, there is an account of Jesus' healing a blind man. Jesus' disciples asked him whether the blindness was the result of the man's sin or his parents', and in this case, Jesus said that neither had caused this man's blindness. In fact, some of our problems are not inherited, and there are times when physical conditions occur that are seemingly random happenings in the mystery of nature.

When it comes to the attitudes, behaviors, and habits that keep us separate from each other and God, however, we do affect each other. Once you become aware of your own part in a dynamic that is perpetuating a system destructive to your own life and destructive to others, you become responsible for changing the dynamics. The kindest thing we do for each other is to clean up our patterns of dysfunction so that we do not inflict them on others or pass them down to others.

Jesus' words in Matthew, when understood to be applicable to the inner kingdom of the parental complexes, is profound and life-altering: "Anyone who loves his father or mother more than me is not worthy of me; anyone who loves his son or daughter more than me is not worthy of me, and anyone who does not take up his cross and follow me is not worthy of me. Whoever finds his life will lose it, and whoever loses his life for my sake will find it" (Matthew 10:37-39).

To be free and to live with autonomy and authenticity, it is necessary to stop being driven by the inner parental complexes and to take up the cross of one's own authentic and unique life.

James Hollis asks the question, "And what would it feel like if one were to operate out of the natural core of one's being? We do so act, occasionally, at least, when we are most spontaneous or wholly in that moment."

"Tell me, what is it you plan to do with your one wild and precious life?" the poet Mary Oliver asks ("The Summer Day," *Selected Poems* [Boston: Beacon Press, 1992]).

Jesus of Nazareth said, "Come unto me, all you who are weary and heavy-laden, and I will give you rest. Take my yoke upon you, and learn of me, for my yoke is easy and my burden is light" (Matt 11:28-30).

The complexes are yokes, breaking the necks and spirits of persons made in the image of God.

When Jesus asked, "Who is my mother?" he was, in a sense, separating himself from his earthly mother. We must do that, as well, and we must separate ourselves from the complexes. Taking on the yoke of Christ is taking on the yoke of love, and in that love is freedom.

"What's going on?" I asked Christy, a new directee. She is a recovering alcoholic and has worked hard at her recovery. She asked me to be her spiritual director because, as she said, she wanted to take her recovery deeper into her spiritual life.

"I've been practicing a new behavior all week since I saw you," she told me. Her eyes were shining and she had a huge smile on her face, a face that used to convey pain and sorrow. "I've made up my mind not to let my new behavior scare me back into my old patterns."

Two years ago, while sitting on a podium at Bonhomme Presbyterian Church in St. Louis, Missouri, I had my usual pre-sermon jitters before the morning worship service that was to conclude a weekend conference on contemplative prayer. Listening to the introduction someone gave for me, a radical, new thought danced lightly across my mind.

"What if I believed what that person is saying about me? What if I started listening to that voice of affirmation instead of the voices of my complexes? What if I started being the person they think I am?"

I was reminded of a prayer I'd seen on a poster years before that said, "God, please help me to accept your opinion of me, no matter how good it is."

What if we lived with each other—connecting, relating, joining together—as persons made in the image of God, beloved sons and daughters in whom the Parent is well pleased?

Questions for Reflection and Discussion

1. Describe a time when you "just weren't yourself." What happened? What did you say that either surprised you or that you regretted? What were you feeling? How did you feel afterward?

2. Describe a time when you changed your behavior, at the risk of losing the approval of someone you care about. What was the outcome?

3. Describe a relationship with someone that repeatedly has outcomes you don't like. What keeps you from making changes that would change the outcome of those encounters?

4. There's an old saying from a poster: *Wherever you go, there you are.* What does that mean for you?

5. Are you more worried about displeasing God or your earthly parents? Explain.

Taking Action

1. Read the Psalms. Underline every verse about God's love and care. *Think on these things.*

2. Make a list of qualities you need in a good inner father. Be aware of how you talk to yourself. Upgrade the behavior of your inner father toward you. Determine to be a better father to yourself.

3. As you listen to speakers, teachers, and preachers, notice if the messenger has a delivery that empowers the listeners, overpowers them, or disempowers you. Make conscious choices about those who have input in your thinking. Make sure it is consistent with who you want to be.

Jesus, the Masculine, and Me

"When you announce that you are woman, do you always have to roar?"

—Cartoon male to a female

May the Lord make your love increase and overflow for each other and for everyone else. . . . May he strengthen your hearts so that you will be blameless and holy in the presence of our God and Father . . . .

—1 Thessalonians 3:12-13

The quality of all of our relationships is a direct function of our relationship to ourselves. . . . The best thing we can do for our relationships with others, and with the transcendent, then, is to render our relationship to ourselves more conscious.

—James Hollis

What women want is what men want. They want respect.

—Marilyn vos Savant

Everyone has power.

Men and women have inherent power, based on particular personal attributes, and some have power derived from position or privilege. Some power is earned; some power is inherited; and some power is seized. Some folks assume power that doesn't really belong to them, and sometimes that works and sometimes it doesn't. Having the wrong person "in power" can wreak havoc on a family, an organization, or a nation.

We are born with power, and if you doubt that, remember a time when a week-old, seven-pound infant could keep an entire household up and awake all night long?

Human beings use power wisely for the good of others, and some overpower others, abusing what they have been given to harm and hurt others. Some people empower others and some people disempower others.

Some power is born of weakness and dysfunction. How often families or systems are controlled by the "weakness" of one person's character defect! How often it is that the seeming victim in a system is actually the persecutor, while the apparent persecutor is the actual victim! How can you ever figure out who's to blame?

Some use anger and fear to gain power over others, intimidating people they say they love with abusive words and actions. Is there anything more powerful than the cold violence of silence? Does anything shred another's feelings of well-being more than being shunned and ignored?

Who hasn't known the debilitating effects of passive aggression, covert control and manipulation, power that sneaks out through lies, half-truths, and "crazy-making" talk and behavior?

Power is energy, and it is neither inherently good nor bad. All humans have power of different kinds and in different degrees, and what we do with our power not only reveals who we are but shapes the quality of our lives.

There is power that lies within our masculine strengths and power that lies within our feminine strengths, and each of us, male and female, has a responsibility to be a good steward of those powers, learning how to use them wisely and well. The masculine and feminine strengths within us may fight for power just as outer men and women do. Sometimes logic overwhelms intuition, and at times the heart takes over the head! Becoming conscious of how those inner powers interact and learning the agenda of each can change a person's life.

In a recent cartoon strip, Crankshaft's grandson asks him if he has ever been able to figure out women.

"All I know is that they have a different game plan than we do," the crusty old curmudgeon responds. "That's why they call it an agenda gap."

We all have an agenda as we go about our daily tasks, and I'm noticing that those agendas are as varied as the individuals. Instead of our needs, desires, and agendas being fixed in time, always the same for men or always the same for women, I've noticed that those inner drives fluctuate, sometimes from moment to moment. Where two or three persons are gathered together, there will be an agenda gap! And where two or three persons meet, part of the agenda is about power.

On a hot summer day when I was ten years old, I learned an important lesson about gender relations and boundaries. I was riding in the back seat of our car with my sister and brother-in-law on a long stretch between New Mexico and California.

My parents, in the front seat, had had a discussion about which shirt my dad would wear that day, and after they talked things were a little tense. My mother always wanted my father to be dressed in a white shirt and a tie, but on that day he was more interested in staying cool and being on vacation.

Suddenly, my father pulled the car over to the side of the road, got out of the car, opened the trunk, took out his suitcase, and changed his shirt. When he got back in the car, he declared, "No woman is going to tell me what to wear!"

In our family, we told that story from then on, each of us with her own twist to it. While no one said a word on that hot day, and certainly no one laughed then, we always laughed when we told the story later, and no one laughed more than my parents.

Sometimes, we women over-mother other people. I've come to understand that when I do, especially with adults and especially with the men in my life, it's generally because I'm wanting and needing a connection. I've also learned that a lot of what my dad called "meddling" is about staying connected, and I've learned that I need to find more appropriate ways to use my power than meddling.

What happens when a woman does not have appropriate power in a relationship or an organization? Do women abuse power with each other because they have not yet learned how to use power appropriately? Have they been deprived of authentic power and respect for so long that they wield it where they can, however they can?

Are women most cruel to each other, most critical of each other, and most sabotaging of other women's power because they do not feel a sense of internal, personal power? Do women behave badly to each other because they don't know any better or because they are afraid, insecure, angry, or simply power-hungry?

Which woman? Which day?

There is perhaps no teaching of Carl Jung's that has influenced me more than his quote about power. "Where love rules," Jung said, "there is no will to power, and where power predominates, love is lacking."

When it comes to power and gender issues, attitudes and behavior are influenced by the part of the world in which you grew up, your religious upbringing, your temperament, and your family system. The learning tasks for my generation are not the same as for my three adult daughters, and yet both men and women have basic needs and longings.

In his book, *Iron John*, Robert Bly gives a helpful overview of the changing roles of men and women in America and rightly states, I believe, that we all must move forward from the era defined in the 1960s by the various cultural revolutions. Bly writes, "The journey many American men have taken into softness, or receptivity, or 'development of the feminine side,' has been an immensely valuable journey, but more travel lies ahead. No stage is the final stop" ([New York: Addison Wesley Publishing Co., 1990], 4).

Women, too, having accessed their masculine side and developed it, may need to keep traveling to recover a connection with "the deep feminine." Trisha Yearwood sings the complexities and conflicts of today's woman in "Xxx's and Ooo's (An American Girl)":

> She used to tie her hair up in ribbons and bows,
> sign her letters with X's and O's;
> Got a picture of her mama in heels and pearls,
> she's trying to make it in her daddy's world.
> She's an American girl. (from *Greatest Hits,* MCA Nashville, 2007)

It's not easy riding the rapids of change, but it helps to remember that the goal of all of us is what some call "the inner marriage" of the masculine and feminine, a joining of our internal masculine and feminine forces.

In the early 1940s, Maude Merle Masterson, mother of my friend Conrad Masterson, was the first female physician at St. Anthony's Hospital in Oklahoma City. When she began working there, the male physicians told her she would have to use the nurses' lounge since she was female.

The first female professors at Harvard Divinity School described what it was like when they were not allowed to use the faculty lounge. They gathered, instead, in the women's restroom, but when they returned to teach the next semester, that restroom had been shut down. "We were afraid you were going to be subversive," they were told.

In the 1970s and 1980s women were subjected to verbal and nonverbal slights and sometimes outright abuse as they struggled to fulfill their dreams of becoming physicians, professors, and lawyers. Some women, in order to survive, became stuck in a masculine mode and have trouble getting out of it; it is as if the masculine strengths are a protective shield, a defense a woman is sometimes unwilling or afraid to surrender.

Only last week my daughter entered a hospital room to check her new patient, a newborn. The father of the new mother referred to Julie, the attending pediatrician, as "a friend of my daughter."

When he started out of the room, he noticed her badge and said, "Oh, I didn't realize you were the nurse."

Julie told me this, laughing, and then she said, "I didn't even bother to address it; it wasn't worth it."

I asked her if it bothered her, and she shrugged it off. Some of her colleagues, she said, would have been offended and would have made sure the father knew his mistake. Julie said, "I think it's a temperament thing, Mom." I would like to think she is so secure in herself as a person and a physician that she didn't need to make an issue of it. Knowing her as I do, I am confident that she can stand up for herself!

All of us need our masculine strengths in order to get through life. Being conscious of those strengths and knowing how to use them is one of the keys to effective living. Masculine strengths help us make decisions and run an orderly civilization. It is the masculine strengths that set rules and limits, structures, laws, parameters, guidelines, and procedures. Masculine strengths give us focus and clarity, help us act independently and with self-reliance. They provide us with rational and logical thought processes and facilitate procedures. When you know the rules, it's easier to get through life.

Masculine strengths are also about power, control, action, results, and tasks. What's not to like about that?

There was a time when I joked about being my husband's personal holy spirit. Trying to recover from being a meddling woman who makes helpful suggestions and leaves hints through the books I leave on the lamp table, books that I think my husband needs to read "for his own good," I signed up for a course on masculine psychology at the Jung Center. I wanted to learn about men, but I was also interested to see what I could discover about my own masculine side. The course was also research for this book.

It was a large class, composed of a balance of men and women, and each week, James Hollis taught the class, using his book, *Under Saturn's Shadow*, as his primary text but always adding important and helpful information. Throughout the class, I thought repeatedly, "I wish I had known this years ago."

It was a sobering class, and people were sober in it, listening intently to an expert talk about the state of men in our culture, their fears and needs, their loneliness and isolation and our culture's complicity in keeping men bound in behaviors that work against the health, maturing, and wholeness of men.

Whether you are a man or a woman, you have three important responsibilities when it comes to those masculine strengths.

- Every one of us is responsible for managing our strengths so that we do not overpower or disempower someone else.
- Every one of us is responsible for being clean and clear with our power issues so that our power does not come out in passive aggression, manipulation, or control.
- Every one of us has an inner male, or several of them, sometimes acting as a loving father, but often behaving as a critical, judging parent, telling us, "You didn't do that right," or "You can't do anything right." That inner voice, the voice of the father complex, can tyrannize the most sophisticated man or woman, rendering him or her paralyzed with fear and self-hatred.

Within the same week, I had two stunning experiences.

At lunch on a warm summer day, I sat across from a good friend, a male lawyer, and heard him express his perspective, opinions, feelings, and thoughts about what it is like for a man in today's world. To say that my friend was passionate about what he was telling me would be an understatement; in fact, it took me several attempts to convince him that I *understood* what he was saying and, as much as possible, his frustration.

I had just read the book *Good Will Toward Men*, in which author Jack Kammer addresses some of the same questions and issues my friend expressed.

How does it hurt male/female relationships to say and believe that "men have all the power"?

Is asking a woman to acknowledge her part in a problem the same thing as "blaming the victim"?

Why are some women afraid that men really might "express their feelings"?

Do women harbor attitudes of superiority over men?

Krammer says that men are "absolutely terrified in the office" because they are so afraid of claims of sexual harassment. He says, "And women wonder why men aren't respecting the rules. Basically, the rules haven't been defined. And neither men nor women understand what is going on."

Later, my feminist friend hooted at what I'd heard from my lawyer friend and at the premises of Krammer's book. "Men have had the power, and they don't like sharing it. They've abused women over millennia; I don't feel sorry for them."

Using her masculine strengths, she continued to argue her point, and I realized that there would be no dialogue. I decided to change the subject.

It is hard to change our paradigms, isn't it? It's hard to find balance within our inner lives, and the less balance we have internally, the less we will have externally. We fight outer battles when we should be seeking peace within! We often assume a position and then defend it long past the time it is necessary to do so.

The second stunning experience happened within hours after these two conversations. The news made *USA Today* and other major newspapers across the country. Southwestern Baptist Theological Seminary in Fort Worth, Texas, would begin offering homemaking classes for the wives of the ministerial students. As I read the news release, I found that I was holding my breath. I almost couldn't believe what I was reading.

The "Women's Studies" program at the seminary from which my father and husband graduated teaches women to do "woman to woman" ministry. The course descriptions on the website indicate a goal of teaching women the "biblical model" of womanhood, a model based on the idea of male superiority and the need for women to submit to their husbands.

In the first place, the announcement that home economics classes are being taught at this graduate school of theology was embarrassing to those of us who are a different kind of Baptist. Being the brunt of societal ridicule has gotten old. Upon reflection, I had two other equally strong reactions.

I am appalled that homemaking classes and this hierarchical system of family life is being taught at what was once a respected institution of higher learning. I realize that in some areas, anti-intellectualism is in, but that doesn't make it a good thing. This seminary is a *graduate school.* Through the years, brilliant professors inspired students to think in that graduate school. What have we come to, I wondered, if they are teaching homemaking?

On another level, however, I am saddened by the fact that in many ways, the arts of making a home and nurturing and caring for children have been neglected just as the feminine strengths have been neglected.

Amy, my youngest daughter, has two Master's degrees, but chose to stay home with her young sons for the first few years of their lives because she believed that staying home was important. I know she is telling me the truth when she describes how people respond when they meet her because I have observed that reaction from "working" women to stay-at-home moms. "It's as if I vanish," my daughter says.

Today's young girls are encouraged to be athletes and compete, and there is nothing wrong with that. They have been pushed to excel in math and science, and that is a good thing. At the same time, tasks that mothers have passed down to their daughters and granddaughters throughout history are no longer valued.

As woman have advanced in becoming free of role constraints and broken through glass ceilings to accomplish amazing feats, many have left their feminine qualities behind. Having tasted freedom from the drudgery of housework and the exhilaration of achieving, accomplishing, and acquiring power and position, women are also experiencing some of the same health problems that men have had. They are working double shifts, at home and at work, and in their push for liberation, power, and success, sometimes lose their natural, instinctual feminine strengths.

Over the last few months, I've had numerous conversations with women about what it means to "access your masculine side" in order to become more balanced. Initially, someone in the conversation goes to an extreme example, pointing out women who dominate others and are "patriarchal" women, women who primarily express masculine strengths. Frankly, I understand; I've been on the receiving end of the aggression of patriarchal women, and I don't like it!

I hear a great deal more criticism of each other than praise and support of each other, and often women express distrust of other women. When I ask such questions as "Do women handle power poorly?" or "Do women behave better toward each other when they have authentic power?" and "Why are women so hard on each other?" inevitably, I hear a story of the misuse of power. "Men are just more honest," women sometimes say, and I have to say, "Well, it depends on *which men* you're talking about!"

In those conversations, I listen carefully for the differentiation between roles women play and qualities they exhibit in whatever roles they are fulfilling. Within the same week, I talked with two women whose careers constantly place them in situations formerly held by men. Fascinated, I listened to a Houston policewoman talk about her job, and it was clear to me that her feminine strengths, in her words, were her greatest assets in dealing with some of the most difficult situations a law enforcement officer could imagine.

Over several days, I talked with a close friend, Susan Garner, a female corporate executive in a male-dominated profession who has risen to the top of her company by being an excellent listener, a consensus builder, and a fabulous hostess. Sitting in her apartment on the 23rd floor of a high-rise in New York City, I reflected on the ways in which she moves freely back and forth between masculine and feminine strengths with facility and poise. She can be warm and nurturing and clear and concise at the same time, and it seems effortless and graceful.

A woman who has access to both sides of her brain and both aspects of her strengths is a wondrous being to behold! Men who are comfortable with their own masculinity and are able to access their feminine sides, as well, seem to have a peace and a naturalness about them. They have access to their feelings. They are powerful, but do not overpower others and can share power with others.

For some women, being comfortable expressing masculine strengths is a matter of geography; where you grew up matters. For the most part, women who grew up in the North don't understand the reservation and hesitation of Southern women. To them, the "velvet-covered brick" seems dishonest, hypocritical, and manipulative. To Southern women, women who grew up in the north or the west are perceived as being pushy, aggressive, and outspoken. Again, which woman are we talking about?

Women and men in different generations approach the issues of expressing masculine strengths differently, and as I listen to conversations, I am convinced that along the way toward liberation, there have been both gains and losses. Who your role models were matters as well.

Religious beliefs shape how a woman feels about her masculine strengths and the choices she makes, as do natural temperament and life experience. I've had a hard time coming to grips with my own masculine strengths. Sometimes, I've been afraid of speaking up, asserting myself, and acting independently, often because I've not wanted to be called by the names given to aggressive women. As I talk with other women, I realize that I'm not alone in my reservations. Many women hold back out of fear of being perceived as bossy or "animus possessed."

Who could have imagined that it would be Jesus who would help me?

Actually, I've had a bit of a checkered past with Jesus.

When I was a young child, growing up in a preacher's home in Texas in the 1950s and '60s, I didn't respond too well to some of the messages I got in church. Looking back, I realize now that it wasn't *Jesus* who gave me trouble so much as it was some of his press agents. Some of the people in my history were a lot more concerned about following the rules and *being good* than about loving each other.

I shudder to this day when I recall an incident when I was fourteen and had invited the girls in our church to see the movie *South Pacific*. The church lady who took us to the movie was horrified by what she saw, and she immediately went to my father to report my bad influence. From then on, she tattled on me with great delight.

My father's life had been radically altered as an adult by a transformational experience he had in Tucumcari, New Mexico, an experience that forever changed the course of our family's history. Ultimately, his good common sense, sane theology, and passionate love for what he called the centrality of Christ was stronger than the negative voices of my childhood. There was something authentic and powerful about my father's love for Christ, and that finally triumphed over the other in the world of my childhood religion, but it's taken some work to get there.

Earlier, and to my dad's credit, he defended me when some of the women in the church went to him out of concern for my soul because I, the preacher's daughter, had not "walked the aisle" by the time I was eight. My dad informed them that I would do that in my own time, but nevertheless, I felt the pressure to invite Jesus into my heart and be baptized. I did not want my parents to be embarrassed.

Frankly, some of the language of religion bothered me, and as an adult I've struggled to use language that makes sense. When I was pregnant with my second child, my three-year-old daughter Michelle came running to me, asking, "Mommy, Mommy, it is Jesus in your heart and the baby in your tummy, or the other way around?" Sometimes, our theology gets trapped in our language.

The heavy emotionalism of revival meetings felt oppressive to me; even then, I resisted the pressures to conform to an external motivation, and even then I knew there was something more to being saved than being kept out of hell and admitted to heaven in the afterlife. I also knew early and deeply that spirituality was about more than simply keeping the rules.

When I was about eight years old, I went with my mother and some of the women of the church to a women's gathering at Glorieta Conference Center. My mother had written a song for the center, and there was a lot of excitement about the week. As we walked into the large meeting room, I spotted a huge banner at the front. Emblazoned on that banner in large letters were the words, "Christ is the answer."

"What's the question?" I asked, and my mother quickly silenced me. I'm *confident* that at that point, I was being honest and not sassy, though I was and am perfectly capable of being sassy.

Through my college years at Baylor University, I was drawn to serious discussions about matters related to faith and the working out of the Christian message in real life. In fact, it was the penetrating question on a poster for Religious Emphasis wee, taped to the elevator in my dorm, that grabbed my attention as I hopped on the elevator right before curfew. I was riveted to the question posed by Jesus to Peter, "Who do *you* say that I am?"

I pondered the question as I rode the squeaky elevator all the way to the sixth floor of Ruth Collins Hall, and it is that question that has shaped much of the quest of my adult life. I am confident that the serious intellectual grappling with that question both protected me from sentimental religiosity and moved me toward meaningful and deep encounters with the Living Christ.

My husband finished seminary and began his ministry on college campuses just as the Jesus Movement was peaking. I couldn't bear the casual talk about Jesus, the T-shirt and bumper sticker theology, Jesus yells and Jesus rallies. When people said, "Praise the Lord," it often sounded flippant to me. When zealous Jesus people asked me if I were "totally committed" or if I "had the Spirit," it was as if I were struck dumb. I wanted to ask them what they meant, but I knew that if I did it would appear that I wasn't a "true believer."

Only today, decades later, I led a discussion about Nicodemus in a Bible study, and woman after woman expressed her discomfort with the term "born again." That a process that is so sacred, so important and meaningful, and so *hard* as rebirth, transformation, and salvation has been misused, abused, overused, and misunderstood is for some of us embarrassing and for others off-putting.

Through the years, as well, I've noticed that within the Christian community, "being a Christian" has come to mean something far different from what I believe it to mean. For some, being a Christian is about following the Ten Commandments or the rules, some of them spoken and some of them not, and for others, increasingly, being a Christian is nothing more than having a particular political point of view.

I will always be grateful for the teachers who expanded my mind about Jesus, starting with the influence of professors and speakers who spoke about Jesus and matters of religion out of good scholarship and balanced thinking.

For decades, I listened to my husband's preaching and teaching about Jesus, and it was his scholarship and meaningful applications that began to give substance and import to the life of Jesus for me. His teaching was so important to me that I began to study the life and teachings of Jesus for myself, and that intellectual quest moved me deeper into a healthy and sane view of the historic Jesus and the risen Christ.

Finally, it was contemplative prayer and using my imagination to enter the Gospel stories that completed the turnaround for me. Over time, both my mind and my heart were engaged and I began to understand and know as I had not known before.

On a hot summer day at Laity Lodge in the Hill Country of Texas, I sat toward the back of the Great Hall and listened to Keith Hosey give the guidelines for our "day in the desert," the day in which we would be in silence. This early morning gathering would be the last one of our group for twenty-four hours. It was Keith's custom during those life-changing contemplative weeks to develop a theme throughout the week, and the day of silence was to be a day of going deeper into the silence. I would have gone to that retreat each year just for that day of silence in that sacred place.

"I want you to imagine Jesus as your big brother today," Keith said, "and as you go throughout the day, imagine that he is taking you on an adventure."

It's always been easy for me to use my imagination, especially when it comes to worrying and picturing bad things happening. As soon as I heard

Keith's instructions, I was captivated, but then I hit a speed bump, trying to imagine Jesus as a big brother.

As the youngest of three daughters, I'd always wanted a big brother. I envied my friends whose big brothers watched over them, teased them, and took them places, and so I thought Keith's idea was going to be good, if only I could get past the images of Jesus from Sunday school pictures of my childhood.

Keith dismissed us for our day in the desert, but I sat in the Great Hall, wondering how I could possibly do what he asked. Suddenly, looking toward the front of the Great Hall, I had my inspiration. Keith was standing with Howard Hovde and Eddie Sears in front of the large stone fireplace. If I could have had a big brother, I thought, I would have wanted a composite of these three men. Suddenly, my imagination had something with which to form an image of Jesus as my elder brother.

Once I became aware of the power of using imagination in prayer, I could begin to reconstruct my image of God and my image of Jesus, and once that began to happen it was as if I no longer needed the images. Gradually, I began to understand experientially what Jesus meant when he defined eternal life as *knowing him* (John 17:3) and when he said, "I no longer call you slaves; I call you *friends*" (John 15:15).

I wrote *Becoming Fire* using various scenes in the Gospels to enhance the reader's use of imagination to experience the presence of Christ. Using the various encounters, I wrote about imagining yourself as one of the characters in the stories, and then imagining what it was like for Jesus to look you in the eye, speak to you, heal you, and love you.

After several years of teaching this method at retreats, it occurred to me to imagine what it was like to be the human Jesus, and so I began including that process in the retreats I led. The process was so meaningful that I decided to work up a book proposal. Twelve publishers turned down *Christheart*, saying that their readers weren't ready for that much of the human Jesus, but Smyth & Helwys had the courage to give me a "yes" and a contract. It was then that I really got in trouble.

As I was trying to write *Christheart* I was also facing the four biggest problems I had ever had. These problems were so big and so potentially heartbreaking for me that it felt as if they had moved in and taken over my life. I remember praying in the middle of the night, alone in my living room, "God, please be bigger in my mind than these problems. Please save me from these problems!"

At the time, I was seeing Sister Mary Dennison for spiritual direction. I would pour out my heart to her and then say, "Sister Mary, how can I write this book on Jesus? I have these problems that I cannot solve. Who am I to write anything about Jesus, given my circumstances?"

I have said that Sister Mary is the embodiment of equanimity, and as I poured out my feelings and tears, she would listen patiently. Always reassuring, she continued to encourage me, and one day, she spoke words that were like healing balm on my trouble soul. "Jeanie," she said, "how can you write about the suffering savior if you haven't suffered, too?"

I did not like what she said. I wanted her to give me an answer, a quick fix, a remedy, or a painkiller. I wanted her to tell me that I could call my publisher and tell them that I simply could not fulfill my contract. Firmly, faithfully, Sister Mary stuck to her guidance, and so I gathered up my anguish and went home to my computer.

Every morning, generally after still one more upsetting phone call related to one of my four problems, I gathered my commentaries and my Bible around my computer. As I waited for my computer to boot up, I would pick up the small wooden bowl that Jan Hiland had given me and remember her words to me.

"Before you write each day," Jan had told me, "feel the emptiness of this bowl. Let it remind you to empty yourself before you start writing. Ask God to fill the emptiness so that you aren't writing just what you want to write, but what God inspires you to write."

Day after day, I would do this, and then I would abandon myself into the hands of God. I would pore over the text for that day's writing. I would read my commentaries and I would sit in the silence, and then I would put my fingers on the keyboard, not knowing what would come from my mind and heart, through my fingers, and onto the screen.

Each day, however, as the words began to flow, making sentences and paragraphs and pages, suddenly it was as if a strength beyond myself would take over the process. Identifying with the human Jesus in my writing, I felt that I had become focused and centered. Imagining myself as Jesus, admittedly an outrageous act and a potentially dangerous thing to do, I found an inner courage and boldness I had never experienced before. Fortunately, my ego was strong enough to know that I wasn't really Jesus, but if it hadn't been, my life was letting me know! That I was experiencing an egocide was without question; I've learned that ego gives up very slowly, perhaps in thin layers.

In telling this story, I have said that it was then that I began to understand just how it is that "Jesus is the answer."

In the coming months and years, that experience would lead me to a journey I could not have imagined as I began to discover the masculine strengths within my inner landscape. I could not have imagined how difficult the process of "finding my inner male" and becoming good father to myself would be.

A couple of years after moving to Houston in 1992, I had a terrifying dream. The dream bothered me a lot, but at the time, I had no one who could help me interpret it or, as dream analysts say, "work the dream." Seven years later, I dreamed the same dream again with a slight variation. As I lay with my heart pounding, caught midway between the dream world and the outer world, I knew the dream had huge meaning for me.

That dream propelled me into the process of Jungian analysis. Trained to understand the ways in which the Dream Maker works, depth analysts guide the dreamer to look for the meaning in the symbols, the message in the dynamics of the dream figures, and the revelations of the True Self, the complexes, and other parts of the psyche. It was also in that process that I first heard Christ referred to as the symbol of the Self. Hearing that terminology, I realized that integrating the biblical Jesus into my inner world, imagining his presence with me and as an inner voice was another way of talking about "inviting Jesus into my heart."

Jesus himself defined eternal life in John 17 as "knowing him," and in the original language, that "knowing" is experiential, intimate knowing. Eternal life is about a quality of life, a life "with God." When there is a connection—a joining of forces—of the ego to the inner kingdom, that is being with God. It is practicing the presence of God; it is oneness with God.

Salvation is about wholeness and health in the present moment as well as eternity, and it is far more than keeping us out of hell and getting us into heaven. Salvation is a process that begins with a "Yes!" to an intimate, personal, vital, and dynamic relationship with the Living God who dwells within the human heart.

That scary dream would take me on a journey into the inner kingdom, and in that journey I would go through the process of getting acquainted with my father complex, that portable father within. That dream would guide me to own my masculine strengths as a valid and necessary part of my life.

In the deepest part of my soul and with the deepest reverence, I came to understand what it means that Jesus saves.

Recently, as I was preparing to teach the parable of the Good Samaritan in my Monday night class at St. Luke's United Methodist Church, something wasn't fitting together for me. I'd taught this parable the same way for years, but this time, an inner restlessness was prompting me to keep asking, seeking, and knocking on the doors of the parable. Finally, I went to my bookshelf and pulled down Robert Capon's book, *The Parables of Grace*, and it was then that a new truth opened my mind and heart. It started with a recognition of how seeing *only* the Samaritan as the Christ figure with the call to emulate him in acts of mercy can lead us back to a salvation by works or by fulfilling the law.

How many good works must we do to fulfill the law? Can you become wounded and depleted yourself, caring for others? How many times have I heard people belittle their own worth by comparing themselves to Mother Teresa!

Capon's point that the wounded traveler as one part of the Christ figure and the Samaritan as another part of him resonated with me, and I went to sleep, pondering that interpretation. The next morning, upon awakening, I saw the truth of that parable for my personal journey.

The wounded traveler represents the feminine part of me and the wounded feminine energies in our culture. In a sense, overusing my feminine strengths had led me to codependence, and when I'm in full-blown codependence I, by my own choices, wear myself out.

I'd looked to the church, represented by the priest, to save me as I have served her well and faithfully. I'd looked to "the rules," following the law as represented by the Levite, thinking that if I were "good enough," bad things wouldn't happen to me! Both the institution and legalism, however, simply asked more and more of me, ignoring my wounds. In many ways, both following the rules and serving the institution had exacerbated my condition!

In my world and for a variety of reasons, my masculine strengths had gone underground. They symbolized the disowned part of me, the shadow, the part of me a woman of my culture is not supposed to express just as the Samaritans represent the outcasts of Jesus' day. And yet, it is often in acknowledging, owning, and embracing that which we don't want to admit about ourselves, the disowned and denied parts of ourselves, that we find the balance, the cure, the recovery of our very lives.

It was the masculine strengths in me that picked up my wounded and weak feminine self and took me to a place and a process, the inn, where I could find healing.

The next night, walking the open-minded and open-hearted women in my class through their own analysis of this parable for their lives, it suddenly occurred to me that at still another level of understanding this parable, the innkeeper represents God the Father. The wounded traveler represents God the Son, and the Samaritan represents God the Holy Spirit, out in the world, bringing people back to God. Perhaps the inn is "home," the state of being in which the various parts of ourselves come together at last.

When we go into the Gospel stories with an open mind, engaging the imagination and allowing the wind of the Holy Spirit to blow freely through those stories, that which is old can become fresh and new, and that which was told millennia ago can breathe liberation into our old ways of thinking, our stilted interpretations, and our repetitive patterns that lead us around in circles, tying us up in emotional and relational knots.

How could I ever have imagined that *knowing Jesus* would introduce me to my own disowned shadow, my masculine strengths?

Joining forces is about reciprocity.

My feminine side needs the masculine side in order to express strength and power, and my masculine side needs the openness and receptivity of my feminine side. My inner male needs the intuitive and the emotional that my inner female provides, and the woman in me needs the logic and rational thought that the man in me so loves to give. The feminine and masculine in me need to be able to sing and dance and work well together, with neither overpowering the other.

Questions for Reflection and Discussion

1. Carl Jung said, "Where love rules, there is no will to power, and where power predominates, love is lacking." In what parts of your life do you see this principle at work?

2. Jesus' love healed, transformed, liberated, and empowered men and women. How do power and control inhibit a person from living the abundant life Jesus offered?

3. In what ways do rules, convention, morals, and mores free persons? In what ways do they constrict, constrain, and inhibit the life of a person or an organization?

4. Are you a slave to following the rules? Or, are you in a battle with the rules, constantly challenging authority and those who have authority? What is that like for you? In either case, who's in charge of your life?

5. When have you used your masculine strengths to overpower another person? When have you used those same strengths to empower another?

Taking Action

1. Find persons who are skilled about moving back and forth between masculine strengths and feminine strengths. If you can, interview that person and see if you can discover how that person does it.

2. Find a person you can empower in a way that has integrity for you and truly benefits the other person.

3. Get better acquainted with the ways and means of Jesus. Learn about his way of loving/empowering others.

A Spirituality of the Heart

The best and most beautiful things in the world cannot be seen, nor touched . . . but are felt in the heart.

—Helen Keller

"You will seek me and find me when you seek me with all your heart."

—Jeremiah 29:13

One of the most pusillanimous things we of the female sex have done throughout the centuries is to have allowed the male sex to assume that mankind is masculine. It is not. It takes both male and female to make the image of God. The proper understanding of mankind is that it is only a poor, broken thing if either male or female is excluded.

—Madeleine L'Engle

"Love the Lord your God with all your heart and with all your soul and with all your strength."

—Deuteronomy 6:5

The power to Love is God's greatest gift to man, for it never will be taken from the blessed one who loves.

—Kahlil Gibran

"I'm a spiritual person, but I am not religious," the young man told me as soon as he sat down. "I tried the church, but it didn't work for me."

I have spent my whole life within the structures of organized religion and so I wince when I hear that statement, frequently coming from people working through recovery programs for addictions. I wince because the statement indicates that somehow, the church has not been able to reach that person and be and do for that person what he or she needs. I confess, as well, some defensiveness.

I wince when I hear it because I understand the ways in which the church has failed. I feel both defensive and sad because I've spent much of my time, energy, and effort within the church, attempting to correct that problem.

In order to do find meaning and purpose for the care of my own soul, I have gone outside my tradition to ask, seek, and knock on other doors. I don't know if I've impacted my tradition for the better, but I know that in my quest, I have found enormous meaning and purpose.

"When did you first experience the Presence of God?"

At the beginning of my first year in the Spiritual Direction Institute, I sat with nineteen other people in the library of the Cenacle Retreat Center. Elsewhere on the grounds were the second- and third-year groups. We had all come together for the weekend retreat that signaled the beginning of our year of study together. Gathered in that circle with people with whom I would share hundreds of hours over the next three years, I was convinced that I had been led to this process. With Sister Mary's initial question of us, I was surprised by a memory, long forgotten, that instantly climbed up from somewhere down deep in my archives.

Though I had not thought of this moment in decades, it was as fresh to me on that August day as if I were in that moment. In my sophomore English class at Baylor and through the poetry of T. S. Eliot, I'd learned about kairos time in which you can be present to the past, and yet completely in the present moment. Often, those kairos moments, in which it is possible to experience time past and time present at once, have enormous healing and directional components for the future.

Suddenly, though fully present to Sister Mary and the other retreatants, I was also back in my childhood, swinging on a swing my dad had hung on the one tree in our yard in Lamesa, Texas. We had just moved into the parsonage, a sturdy brick structure next door to the church, and as was his practice when we moved, my father had made sure I could swing.

It was dry in Lamesa, the nights were cool, and the people were warm-hearted and friendly. I loved living there, riding my bicycle on the sidewalks surrounding the church, and eating homemade ice cream after church on Sunday nights in various homes. We called it "after church fellowship," and it was certainly that.

On the hot summer day that emerged from my memory bank, I was alone in my swing, barefoot and carefree and lost in a world of make-believe. Suddenly, the wind shifted and I felt a cool breeze across my face. Holding on to the rope, I leaned back in the swing and looked up into the leaves of the tree and beyond them to the clear blue sky.

That was, I realized, my first experience of the Presence of the numinous, mysterious Force whom I call *God.* Simply recalling that moment now sends a chill up my spine.

Later, when I was fourteen, I was sitting in my bedroom window, this time in the parsonage of the church my dad pastored in Dallas, looking out at the clear, bright full moon. I was full of life and longing, perched on the edge of becoming a woman, and in that moment, it was as if I connected with the Source of life. It was in that moment that I felt that Source beyond myself connected to my own life force. Now, I know that in that instant, I was touching for a moment the deep Feminine.

Still later, as I was doing some work on my birth narrative while attending a retreat at Laity Lodge, I skipped a morning session to go to the track and run. I knew I had some deep and heavy thinking to do. On that morning, it was more important for me to connect with those earliest memories and the voices of my inner child than it was for me to connect with the people on the contemplative retreat, and so I sought sanctuary in that sacred space in the canyon wall overlooking the Frio River. I knew I had an appointment with myself, a divine appointment that God had orchestrated.

We'd been working with our earliest childhood memories all week, and as I ran beneath the gnarled cedar trees, always on the lookout for armadillos or other Hill Country creatures, I kept thinking about my birth. It was as if in the same moment I was where I was, as an adult, but I was also in that hospital nursery, connecting in a mysterious way with myself as a newborn baby, alone and lonely in my isolette.

Seemingly out of nowhere, I suddenly sensed a reassuring Presence, almost like that of God as Mother, hovering over my infant self, rejoicing that I had been born! At the time I did not hear an audible voice, but from that time until this, I have had a sense that God came and got me in that nursery and has never let go. In that moment, I experienced a blessing that I had been craving all of my life, a blessing for who I was.

The meaning I give to all three of those instances is that in each of them, I had a felt sense of my connection to the Source of life itself and a connection to my own soul, the True Self. I cannot prove any of this logically or rationally; I simply know that that felt sense has remained unwavering and constant. If you were to perform surgery and look for the True Self, you could not find it, but I know that it is there, connected with God.

Years later, when I discovered John 15 and the allegory of the vine and the branches as a visual image of how we are connected with God, I knew exactly what the writer of John's Gospel was describing. Instantly, upon reading those verses, I could feel the truth of his words, the accuracy of that metaphor, and the authenticity of my own *spiritual* experiences.

Partly because of those who continue to tell me that they are spiritual and not religious, but also because of the profoundly spiritual experiences I have had in my life, all of them related to nature, I always address the issue of religion and spirituality when I lead retreats and workshops on spiritual growth.

Different people give different definitions, but in my understanding, spirituality is about who we *are.* It is about our life with God, however we image God. We cannot *not* be spiritual. We will have a god because we are inherently spiritual beings. I agree with Carl Jung's concern when he said that we all have gods but the issue is *which* God we choose.

The word "religion" comes from *religare,* which means "to tie or bind ligaments back together." As I understand it, religion is about the things we *do* to bind ourselves back together. Religion has to do with the outward practices and rituals we use to reconnect with our souls and with God.

It is necessary, as well, to differentiate between the institution known as "church," or organized religion, and the living organism, the Body of Christ on earth, in order to understand what role each is to play. Sadly, the institutional church is often more about American capitalism than it is good news, emphasizing size and power more than love and healing. Regretfully, people are often asked to serve the institution when, in fact, the church is intended to serve people and fulfill the mission statement of Jesus, as recorded in Luke 4.

After his baptism and his wilderness experience in which he defined for himself what kind of servant/leader he would be, Jesus returned to his hometown, often the place where it is hardest to be who you really are, and read the following words, taken from the prophet Isaiah. These words define Jesus' mission, and they define what the church is to be doing in the world as the Body of Christ.

> The Spirit of the Lord is on me,
> because he has anointed me
> to preach good news to the poor.
> He has sent me to proclaim freedom for the prisoners
> and recovery of sight for the blind,
> to release the oppressed,
> to proclaim the year of the Lord's favor. (Luke 4:18-19)

Indeed, in much of what goes on in this entertainment-driven era of what is called "church," we have to ask if we are doing what Jesus would do if he were here, or if we are about building kingdoms, providing thrills, or seeking power in a culture where people are poor, blind, and in prisons of their own making.

I am convinced that if Jesus were here today, he would be about the business of healing and transforming us, liberating us, and empowering us to be whole, healthy, and sane human beings. It is not an original thought with me, but I have adopted it as mine when I affirm that at the end of my life I will not be asked if I were like Jesus. Instead, I think that I will be asked if I lived the life I was given to live. Did I become who I really am? Did I live my one authentic, wild, and precious life?

As I reflect on the Jesus story, I am struck repeatedly by the way in which the human Jesus represents the most fully individuated, actualized, and authentic person in history. People argue with me that of course Jesus was all of that, for he was God, after all, but if you accept that he was fully human as well as fully divine, it seems to make sense that he went through the maturation processes of a human person, born a baby and maturing into adulthood.

The more I integrate the Jesus story into the depths of my own experiences, I am increasingly convinced that the masculine and feminine were fully balanced in Jesus. He knew when to express masculine strengths and when to express feminine strengths, and he was comfortable doing what fit the moment's needs.

Jesus was born into a religious world in which people focused primarily on keeping the law, meeting external standards, and practicing the designated rituals of that religious structure, all of which are good solid masculine strengths and practices. What Jesus did was to complete the law by revealing the connecting, loving, joining forces of God. Jesus' life and work was to connect with people; he invited them into relationship with him, and then he taught them how to connect with God by accessing the kingdom within. And when asked about keeping the law, he said that there were only two laws necessary, a scandalous and outrageous claim in a religious world with so many laws that the laws were, Jesus said, "breaking the peoples' back."

Two things are necessary, Jesus said. Love God and love your neighbor as you love yourself. "Love one another," Jesus said, and then he amplified that commandment by saying, "This is how people will know that you are my disciples: by the love that you have for each other."

It's easier, actually, to keep laws and observe holy days, offer sacrifices and give alms than it is to love God, your neighbor, or yourself. It's easier to straighten each other out, point out each other's faults and failings, and build big kingdoms than it is to love with the kind of love that heals, transforms, liberates, and empowers persons to become fully who they are.

My own spirituality was formed in a tradition in which spirituality was graded. Those of us who grew up in my tradition shudder and laugh now at the ways in which we were graded on an "Eight Point Record System" each Sunday. On our offering envelopes, we were to check the boxes if we were present, on time, had studied the lesson, had done our daily Bible reading, brought our Bibles, gave an offering, made a contact with an unchurched person during the week, and attended worship.

There was no way I was not going to make 100 percent on my envelope since I was the preacher's daughter. It was in Sunday school that I first remember lying.

I learned, in this system that emphasized external behavior, rewards, and punishment, that you could be full of deceit, harbor ill will toward others, and do whatever you wanted to and still make 100 percent on the weekly grading system.

Jesus' spirituality was a different kind of spirituality, and he himself said that it begins with a connection to what he called "the kingdom within." When he said we are to seek first the kingdom, I believe one of the things he was saying was that we should connect first with his presence within our inner lives and, in doing that, connect with our own souls as well. Jesus' opinion about this inner world was so strong that he said some of the religious leaders were like whitewashed tombs, clean on the outside but full of decay on the inside.

Jesus' spirituality invites us into a spirituality that is about wholeness and health. Perhaps it is time to revisit some of the feminine strengths and access behaviors that are about inner healing and balance in order to become more authentic men and women. I am convinced that masculine spirituality, which is more about externals, can join forces with feminine spirituality, and that their marriage can be transforming for the individual and then, as a result, for the larger world.

Feminine spirituality is more about process than it is product. It is about relationship more than rules. Feminine spirituality connects us with our own nature, our instinctual energies, and the largeness of nature itself. It is about waking up, becoming aware and fully alive.

Spirituality as Waking Up

In my own journey, I had spent so much time and energy trying to please and placate outer authorities that I had become dead to my life's messages. I knew how to play a role, project an image, and adapt to my environment, but becoming aware of the voices within my inner world was alien to me. Those voices were unavailable to me until they clamored so loudly and insistently that I had to wake up to them, and in waking up to my inner world, I began to wake up to God.

"What is the answer?" I asked upon beginning analysis, and the answer came back over and over, "Awareness, awareness, awareness." I didn't believe it could be that simple, but what I didn't know was how hard something as simple as awareness could be!

Spirituality is about waking up. And waking up some more.

Perhaps even our last transition from this life into the next realm, whatever that may be, is about waking up still more.

Spirituality as Asking, Seeking, Knocking

When I began waking up, it was as if I were set on a journey of discovery and exploration. Instead of being anchored to the old answers, the worn-out patterns, and the rigid belief systems that no longer worked for me, it was as if I were being compelled to ask, seek, and knock about my own life and about God. Pushed out of the boxes that had become too small for me, I was astounded at the ways in which I was seemingly led or drawn to the exact book, teacher, person, or experience that I needed to keep me moving and expanding into the larger world. I began seeing myself and the world and my place in the world. I discovered new truths about God and life that expanded my mind and consciousness. The more I break free of old constraints and explore new horizons and possibilities, the bigger God becomes. For too long, I limited God and my own life.

It was during this stage that I began experiencing vulnerability and a deepening sense of transparency. As I began shedding the old skins of conformity and adaptivity, it was necessary to let go of some connections of the old systems and either reform my new relationships with new ways of connecting or connect with new persons.

Inside my inner kingdom, the negative father tried to scare me about this journey, sometimes trying to pull me back into the old system. Like a newborn, blinking at the bright lights of the delivery room and shivering in the blast of cold air outside the womb, I learned ways to tolerate feeling uncertain and off-balanced, confused and disoriented. I began to learn how to let go, but only gradually, and only as I could, and I learned that only in uncertainty is there really any security.

Near my computer, which is both my workplace and a kind of altar, I keep a quote by Friedrich Nietzsche: "One must still have chaos in oneself to be able to give birth to a dancing star." Sometimes truth is spoken by people who aren't on the reading list for my religious world, and this quote helps me remember that God still hovers over my inner chaos, bringing about form and shape, just as that Spirit hovered over the formless void at creation.

On the journey, I learn to trust God in ways that I can never learn sitting in my safe seats of security, status quo, predictability, and familiarity. On the journey, I have begun to understand that God is not a fixed object, a big man on a throne. God is not a noun, but a verb, and God's verbness reverberates throughout creation, enlivening the universe with creative, life-giving energy.

Spirituality as Partnering and Creating

My insecurity demands that God abide in my self-made doctrines and dogmas; God's goodness refuses to let me stay in the prisons of what-used-to-be, but invites me into a creative partnership. God invites us to join forces and partner with him in creative acts of making a living, creating our lives, and loving each other. Joining forces with the creative activity of

God, we are connected with the same creative force that made the universe. Partnering with God, we are invited to co-create with him.

Instead of standing outside of life, we participate in life and in love and, hopefully, in laughter. We engage with it, experience it, wrestle with its complexities, and work with the stuff of life to bring about something good.

Almost two years ago, I was sitting at the intersection of Buffalo Speedway and Alabama on a cool fall night, reflecting on a conversation I'd had with a woman in the parking lot of St. Luke's United Methodist Church after the Bible study I lead each week.

"What about the abundant life?" this woman had asked, following up on a comment I'd made during the evening. "If abundance means have plenty of the good things, I'm missing out somehow!"

Abundant life is fully engaged living, I thought to myself as the light turned green and I headed toward home. Abundant life is the accumulation of life's experiences, the good and the bad, happy and sad, easy and hard.

Jesus plunged headlong and full-throttle into the human experience, and that is what we are required to do. We can stay adrift in the clouds of theory and ideas, but it is in the muck and mire of life that we experience the abundant life. We can live an orderly religious life, keeping the rules and following the doctrines, but it is in the hard places of loving—really loving with agape love—that we experience the Living God.

There is a childlikeness to this radical spirituality that Jesus modeled, a childlikeness that requires openness, trust, receptivity, and vulnerability. It is a childlikeness that exudes wonder and expresses curiosity. This childlikeness keeps us alive to possibilities, living in the present moment, and open to new experiences, amazing synchronicities, and the sheer joy of being alive. Childlikeness is so important, in fact, that Jesus said that without it, you couldn't enter the kingdom of God.

Spirituality as Abiding

All of us live somewhere, and some of us live in fear. Some of us live in lives too small for our souls, as James Hollis cautions. Some of us live in resentment or jealousy, controlled by guilt or shame, wallowing in hate or anger. Even the most religious persons can live in those shabby dwellings.

We all live somewhere, and we live with other people. *How* we live with others is a direct reflection of how we live with ourselves. It is ourselves, after all, that we live with all the time, and wherever we go, we take ourselves. This different kind of spirituality that springs from the inner world can radically alter the way in which you live with yourself.

In John 1, the Gospel writer recounts an event early in Jesus' earthly ministry in which two of the disciples of John the Baptist were so drawn to Jesus that they left John and began to follow Jesus. Jesus turned around and faced them, asking one of the most important questions of a spiritual journey: "What do you want?" Then he invited the two persons to "come and see" where he lived, how he lived, and what he was about. Jesus invited persons first into relationship with him, and from that primary relationship, everything else would flow naturally.

I've come to understand that when Jesus instructed the disciples to "abide in him," he was inviting them into a radical, life-altering kind of relationship. Living "in God" has always been central in the spiritual life. It has to do not with place so much as it does with an attitude. Writers about the spiritual life have used various terms such as dwelling, resting, and being with God. Dwelling in God creates a relationship that is as close and intimate as the branches are to the vine, and in that intimate connection, it is as if the life of God flows into the person.

I live in the heart of God who lives in my heart is a truth taught by the mystics. *I see the God who sees me. I search for the One who has found me.*

When your religion is about God's being in heaven or *up there*, it is presumed that you have to be good enough or follow the rules well enough to finally make the leap to God or get God to love you. A spirituality of the heart and one I believe Jesus taught affirms that God dwells within us. When the teachers of my childhood were asking me to "invite Jesus into my heart," what they were saying is, "Wake up to the fact that God dwells within you."

Indeed, there is no place we can go where God is not, for God is in all of creation. God is not far away and detached, but present, alive, and active in every moment. Elizabeth Barrett Browning said, "Earth's crammed with heaven, / And every common bush afire with God: / But only he who sees, takes off his shoes / The rest sit round it and pluck blackberries" (*Aurora Leigh*, book 7, lines 821-24).

Feminine spirituality would have us cultivate a sense of God's presence in all things as a gardener would cultivate a garden. Feminine spirituality would call on us to weave new understandings about God into the fabric of our lives. Jesus made references to the work of yeast and making bread; feminine spirituality would "knead" his life into our lives.

Spirituality as Nurturing

"Pay attention to your earliest thoughts upon awakening," James Hollis counseled us in one of the earliest classes I took from him. "When your ego has not yet taken its position as the sentinel on the wall and the unconscious can speak more clearly, you will often see things more clearly."

From the first time I heard that, I have paid attention to those thoughts. I have been astounded by the clarity I have upon first awakening. Sometimes I have a clearer perspective on a problem, an idea for a writing project, or some kind of guidance I'd been needing. Often, when wrestling with a chapter in a book, it is as if what I need is downloaded in the morning when my ego is undefended.

From the moment, I found the image of the vine and the branches in John 15, I have understood God as pouring the nutrients I need into my life as naturally as the nutrients flow from the vine into the branches, producing the fruit that is consistent with the nature of that particular vine.

My part of the nurturing process is to make sure I put myself in a position of receiving what I need, and for me, Centering Prayer is at the core of my spiritual practice. I keep myself in some kind of learning environment all the time, either independently reading or taking classes in order to receive the intellectual nourishment and nurture I need. I tend my family relationships and my friendships carefully, and I engage with my community of faith at a deep level in order to receive the gifts of God through other persons. It is my job to put myself in the places and with the people from whom I can receive nurture; I have discovered that if I do my part, God will do his part.

It is also part of my spiritual practice to nurture others. This is different from keeping others in line. Instead, it is part of my intentional discipline to give what I have been given, to pass on what I have received, to encourage and stir up faith in others, and to love others as I have been loved. I've learned from my AA friends that if you want to keep the abundance of God's nurturing grace, mercy, and love, you have to give it away.

Spirituality as Telling the Stories and Tending the Traditions

In recent years, tradition has fallen on hard times. Younger generations have swept through churches, discarding the old hymns and the old ways and pronouncing them irrelevant to those who pay the bills. It is the job of the young, I know, to breathe fresh life into the world, to carve new paths, and to cooperate with the One who says, "I am making all things new," but it is the job of those who are older to pass on what is good and true from the tradition to the young in such a way that it has life.

Indeed, all of us must be willing to let irrelevant traditions die, and all of us are called to let go of that which is no longer life-giving. We must also stay open to that which is new and fresh without completely cutting ourselves off from our root system, a sure guarantee of death.

I have heard it said that life with God is far too important to keep to oneself, and I take seriously the tasks of consciously passing on the ways and means to those who will come after me. It is important for our children to know the old stories that form the foundation of our life of faith, not only those in the Bible, our sacred text, but those of our collective history. Our young ones need to know why we do certain things the way we do. They need to know that their freedoms of faith were bought on the shoulders of people who came before us all, often sacrificing and sometimes being martyred for their faith.

My son-in-law Jeremy intentionally has chosen mentors for himself, and I admire that. Young and old alike benefit from the exchange of youthful idealism and tested wisdom. Mentoring, modeling, and passing on the traditions are vital ways of keeping connections among persons alive and well. How can our young ones learn how to live together and have faith and courage, stamina and strength if someone doesn't show them?

Spirituality as Transformation

There is enormous difference in a theology that begins with the idea that we are intrinsically *bad,* that we are a zero, and that we have a black heart and a theology that begins with the belief that we are made in the image of God and created just a little lower than the angels, according to the psalmist. I start my theology with the original blessing.

The work of transformation happens within the deepest levels of our souls as the Master Alchemist takes the raw materials of our lives—our natural gifts, our hidden talents, our successes and our failures, our wounds and our brokenness—and works with those various aspects of ourselves *to make us into who we were designed to be.*

In the ways of mystery, God works from within to help us disengage from our ego attachments and engage with the kingdom that is within; God works in mysterious ways to transform our inner lives so that we are no longer bound to limited and limiting ways of being in the world, but are liberated to live the life we have been given.

In the Gospel of John, the writer records what is believed to be Jesus' first recorded miracle, the turning of the water into wine at a wedding party in Cana of Galilee. Over the years, that moment in which Jesus takes a common, necessary element and transforms it into that which symbolizes the sparkle of life has provided me with one of my most valued images.

God can take that which is ordinary and mundane in my life and transform it into something that is full of joy for me and gives joy to others. God can use that which is imperfect, incomplete, and inadequate in me, and in his economy employ all of that raw material to create a richness, depth, and fullness in my life. God can work within the shards of my failures, the fragments of my broken dreams, the messes I've made, the problems I've caused, and the harm I have done to bring about good.

I have learned that there is no end to the grace and mercy of God. God's love is infinite, unconditional, and encompassing. It is also *available.*

Questions for Reflection and Discussion

1. How would you pass on the traditions of what is described in this chapter as "feminine spirituality"? Which ones do you need in your own life?

2. If, as an adult, you assume 100 percent responsibility for your own spiritual and religious life, how can you integrate feminine spirituality into your life?

3. Why is it easier to follow the law than it is to love?

4. For those who haven't had enough structure and stability that the law provides, nurturing may involve giving the foundations of faith. Being a good parents to oneself or others may necessitate providing boundaries, setting limits, etc. Which do you need more, structure or freedom?

Taking Action

1. Attend worship services that are different from yours. Take someone with you and talk about the experience. What needs do the different styles of worship meet? What happens when one style is pushed too far? What is "too far"?

2. Notice what is missing from your own life in terms of your own intellectual, emotional, spiritual, and physical well-being. Take action to take care of that need for yourself. When you need to, ask others for help.

3. Learn something new about music, art, literature, psychology, or religion, if you need that balance, or learn something new about science if that would balance you. Start a physical exercise program if you are sedentary. Plant a garden or tend a plant if you spend too much time indoors and with technology. Volunteer at a non-profit agency. Read a book outside your field. *Do something different!*

Beyond Ourselves: Joining Forces for Community

God is so free of his own creation that he can transform us into a community of people who are able to be free of the very establishments which are formed in his name. For these very establishments begin to institutionalize God's love and then he teaches us . . . what love really is—not our love, not what we want God's love to be, but God's love.

—Madeleine L'Engle

God is love. Whoever lives in love lives in God, and God in him.

—1 John 4:16

The mission for women of which I am speaking here concerns all women, each in her own place. . . . They have the same mission, the reinstatement of the primacy of persons over things. It is in public life and in the cultural sector that this primacy is disregarded most. Hence the importance of women breaking into those sectors, and having their authority in them respected.

—Paul Tournier

One of my favorite cartoon characters through the years has been Dennis the Menace. I love the way he gets important points across, and his travails with Margaret can teach us a lot about our conflicted relationship with "the feminine," those energies that sometimes confound and confuse us even as they rise up from some depths within us, male and female alike.

Recently, Dennis had climbed to great heights in a tree, but looking down at Margaret, he said, "You won't tell anyone you helped me, will you?"

Any one of us, stuck in our masculine strengths of independence and self-reliance, hates to admit that sometimes we need those other strengths, the feminine ones, in order to do certain things in the moment.

"This is not the time to go into your houses and lock your doors. It is a time when we need to join forces and support each other."

It was a cold, gloomy February morning in 1993. I was in a motel room in Waco, Texas, and the television stations were buzzing with the news of the bombing of the World Trade Center in New York City. With chaos in the background, the police chief of the city was pleading with the citizens of New York to move beyond fear to *join together* to get through the crisis.

"When people are afraid," he went on, "it is common to go into their houses and lock their doors and shut themselves off from each other. *This is the time to talk together and to stay in touch with each other.*"

Joining together. Meeting and supporting each other. "Of course that's what we must do," I said to myself, recalling previous inner-city riots and crises when people took to the streets to shoot each other. This police chief was calling for people to go against the grain of their instincts, give up defensiveness and self-protection, move out onto the edge of risk, and stay connected with each other instead of huddling inside, alone and afraid.

Madeleine L'Engle writes in her book, *The Irrational Season*, "God promised to make you free. He never promised to make you independent"([New York: Seabury Press, 1979], 68).

In November after the 9/11 attack in New York City, I sat with my husband at Temple Emmanu El in Houston, listening to Rabbi Marc Gellman and Msgr. Thomas Harmon, "the Godsquad" of ABC News. Each of them had been intimately involved in the crises of that attack, Gellman as the president of the Board of Rabbis in New York and Harmon as a chaplain to the police department. Who would have imagined when these two entertaining and inspiring speakers had been booked for this lecture series that they would be speaking fresh from this tragedy, an event all of us were just beginning to try to integrate into our minds.

Alternately, Gellman and Harmon had us laughing and weeping as they spoke of their "intentional friendship," a phrase that caught my attention. Responding to questions from the audience about what we could *do*, they continued to come back to the same theme: *Make friends with someone different from you.*

That night, I was filled with the desire to *do something,* and the next morning, I woke up with an idea that came to fruition in April 2002 when almost 200 women from eight different faith groups gathered at the church my husband pastors in Houston, River Oaks Baptist, for "A Gathering of Women Interested in Spirituality."

As the guests seated themselves at round tables to facilitate conversation, each table hostess lit a tall white candle in the center of the table, a symbol of peace and hope. As the deacons in our church served dinner, we began to talk to each other with one single intention. We were to get acquainted with each other for the purpose of making friends, understanding each other, and thereby, hopefully, throwing one small pebble in the pond of world peace. Halfway through the evening, we paused in our program to allow the Muslim women to pray; at the end, we sang together, "Let there be peace on earth, and let it begin with me." The evening was electric, and its impact continues even now as women gather together in other houses of faith to know each other and learn about each other's faith.

On Valentine's night, my husband and I went to one of our favorite restaurants in the city, a place where the food is always good, the ambiance is pleasant, and the servers are cordial and helpful. This year, for whatever reason, nothing was up to par, and to make matters worse, we were seated close to two young women whose loud talk and laughter got louder as the evening went on. Their main topic of conversation was "hooking up," and as they used the phrase, I became aware that it was like fingernails on a chalkboard for me.

Relationships, friendships, and community are some of my highest values. I hold the people in my life as if they are a sacred trust to me. I grieve terribly when I have to move away from an important friendship or community or when someone leaves me. Relationships are so important to me that I keep a guard on my own behavior so that I don't cling or overwhelm others. I am aware that my own need for closeness and connection could be stifling or burdensome to others, and so I work hard at respecting others' boundaries. I consciously try not to trespass in others' lives.

These days, there's a lot of "hooking up" in relationships. I understand that mores and morals have changed, but what has not changed is the need of human beings for connections that matter, relationships that nurture and nourish, and communities that provide continuity, stability, and a foundation in which people can experience a meaningful life. Hooking up is often a cheap substitute for making authentic connections, and the repeated practices of casual, dispensable relationships can build habits that prevent people from being able to form and maintain meaningful relationships.

At the heart of the gospel story, as I read it, is the truth of a relational God who was and is intimately involved in creation and wants to be in a loving relationship with each of us. When we are willing to open our minds and hearts to each other, reaching out to each other in acceptance and attempting to understand each other, I believe we participate with God in bringing in the kingdom of love.

To do this, we must move out of our isolation, an isolation made more acute by prejudice and bias, and participate in a spirituality of companionship and community. Both actions go against the grain of our culture, which over-values independence, self-reliance, and looking out for number one. To join forces with each other, we must be intentional and faithful to the nurturing of the holiness of friendship and community.

I cut my teeth on the doctrine of the priesthood of every believer, a doctrine that may need more than a little amplification and explanation in today's world. That doctrine dove-tailed too neatly into a belief, albeit unconscious, that I should be able to handle my own problems, I should be able to work things out on my own, and I should keep a stiff upper lip, hold things close to the chest, and not complain. Frankly, that set of rules almost killed me!

How liberating it has been to experience the healing power of talking things over with someone who understands that the life of the soul needs to be tended. The voice of the soul and the suffering of the soul need to be heard by someone who cares. Through the Twelve Steps, I've experienced the freeing acceptance of the spirituality of imperfection. Through my work with my spiritual directors and wise analysts, I've come to experience what it means to be valued, heard, and accepted, no matter what. In the sacred acts of friendship, I've experienced the joys of companions who are also on the path of the soul's journey.

In companioning, no one person is "the leader," but there is a sharing of the journey from a position of equality and mutuality. There is reciprocity in companioning, a give and take that keeps a holy balance in the relationship, and in that give and take, there is a depth of respect for the ways in which the Spirit of God moves and shakes things up instead of judgment or censure.

I'm still in process and I hope that will be my pattern for the rest of my life as I transition from one season to another, letting go of what no longer serves my life and staying open and receptive to the One Who Makes All Things New, even when what comes to me is hard. I've made peace with the fact that I will never arrive. I'll never know all the answers or even all the questions, and while excellence is an option in this daring adventure called life, perfection is not. Perfection is, in fact, a slow death, says writer and minister Hugh Prather, and I know that he is right. I pray that as I grow older I can resist less and cooperate more with life's gifts, holding them with reverence, even when they are first obscured by darkness.

I want to live in community with fellow travelers who are willing to be less concerned about outer appearances, keeping the law, and striving for external reward and are more concerned with joining in relationships that are meaningful and intentional.

I've given up the idea that I can earn God's favor or rewards by my good behavior or good works not because I wanted to but because life has demanded that of me. I'm more concerned about loving God for love's sake and trusting God in the midst of whatever is. I'm not so interested in how things look on the outside, and I don't swoon over external deeds, mine or others', but I am interested in experiencing the presence of God within and seeing, celebrating, and sharing the presence of God in others, even when they do not look like me.

Because of my life's work, I do a lot of proclaiming, telling, and declaring, and sometimes I wonder when the day will come when I will put my hand over my mouth or take my hands off the keyboard and say, "I've said it all." I'm not there yet, but I do know that in this pilgrimage, listening, hearing, and receiving are of vital importance, and the most crucial listening I do is listening in the silence, for it is there that God speaks most eloquently. Silence is, after all, God's first language. It is important that we, God's instruments, God's friends, learn that language.

I love to learn and study. On my desk is a small paperweight with the words of Michelangelo, "I am still learning," but more than knowing facts and certainly more than piling up information, I'm interested in meaning. I want to take the wisdom of the world and knead it into my own life so that when I need it, it is there, waiting to be used for good in my life or another's. God still speaks in many languages and through different voices, and I want to hear as many of those voices as possible so that I can know the largeness of God.

I like to be right and certain, but more and more I'm understanding that there is more than one point of view, and we humans always see through the glass darkly, just as the Apostle Paul did. I've learned that there is cold comfort in being *certain*, for the next step over from certainty is arrogance; about the time I think I've gained the corner on truth, something I've never imagined interrupts my prideful strut and shows me that certainty is for God. Besides, human certainty has a way of separating human beings from each other; certainty drives us to our holy huddles where we speak the same jargon to each other. *How can we be salt and light in the world God loves if we hide in our religious ghettos?*

"It is as if the first half of life, others write your biography," Pittman McGehee says frequently. "In the second half of life, life hands you the pen and invites you to write your *auto*biography." I know that he must repeat this admonition because it is so hard for us to take responsibility for our lives and become our own authorities.

James Hollis echoes the urgency of this task of life when he cautions us to beware of those who would assume authority for us. We must run fast in the other direction when someone assumes that power position of external authority and says, "Listen to me. I'll tell you what to believe. You'll be safe if you do what I say, believe what I teach, follow my teachings."

Instead, each of us must come to bear the terrible burden and gift of listening to the kingdom of God within if we are to be free and authentic. We are not, after all, automatons or robots; we are persons made in the image of God and granted the freedom to choose.

In this different form of spirituality, we don't assume to tell the Deity what to do or how to run the universe. We don't insist on special favors just for our tribe, our family, our country. Instead, prayer becomes a communion with God in which we attempt to listen to God. Prayer in this feminine mode is about waiting, staying open and receptive, listening, and then moving in cooperation with God's spirit. It is seeking to discern where the Spirit is moving and then moving with it.

Like a child, I often bring my prayer requests to God. I plead with God for the things I want, but more and more I'm seeing prayer as God's praying to us, asking us to work with him, move with him, cooperate and partner with him as he brings life and love, healing and help to others.

In my prayers, I'm more often asking, "God, what is it you want me to see in this situation?" and "What am I missing here?" I ask God more questions than I tell him what to do, and that shift in attitude from asking to telling seems to free me up to trust the Almighty with what I sometimes feel I cannot bear. Increasingly, my prayer is, "Thy will be done."

This different kind of spirituality seems to me to fit a postmodern era. It seems to me to reflect a move from a concept of God as rule-giver, judge, and jury to an experience of God as Lover, Friend, Advocate and Guide, Helper, Physician, Living Water, and Bread of Life. When persons know God as Love, then the natural consequence of that is to extend that love to others, building a community of grace and mercy.

I have few delusions about community life. I am confident that there are few things that bring out the raw edges of a human being more than getting too close for comfort. If it weren't so hard, I suppose, more people would be doing it.

Perhaps that is the growing edge for us as a family of faith, and perhaps we are being called to go to the hard places, explore the rough edges, refuse to be defeated by the hate and fearmongers, and learn what it means to live together in harmony and peace. As followers of Christ, perhaps it is time for us to review his teachings and figure out what he meant us to do and be.

"I'm a Christian," the man told me as we rode the MARTA together across Atlanta. "I follow the Ten Commandments and I want them posted in every courtroom in America."

"But the Ten Commandments are in the Old Testament, " I said tentatively, wondering if this was one of those times when I needed to keep my mouth shut. "How about posting the Sermon on the Mount?"

The man looked at me as if I were speaking a foreign language, and returned to his *Sports Illustrated* Swimsuit Edition.

I am convinced that we can be intentional about forming community, joining forces, and that we must be. I am convinced that community is a sacred responsibility and that learning how to live together as brothers and sisters in the global family is our collective growing edge.

At the end of January 2008, my husband and I joined 10,000 or more fellow Baptists at the convention center in Atlanta for a gathering of

Baptists called by President Jimmy Carter. The intention of the meeting was reconciliation, and, as Marv Knox of the *Baptist Standard* wrote, "to push back the cursed darkness of racism that enshrouded Baptists in this hemisphere for 160 years" ("Candles alight for new Baptist unity," *Baptist Standard*, February 18, 2008).

For two and a half days, we joined forces with several other Baptist groups, dove-tailing with the various members of the National Baptist Convention. We sang and heard music that made chills run up and down my spine. We heard speeches so inspiring and stimulating that if there had been an altar call, I would have "walked the aisle" more than once. It had been a long, long time since I'd been proud of being a Baptist, so dismal and dark have been the news reports and happenings for thirty years; this was the best meeting I've attended in ages.

With Jesus' mission statement in Luke 4 as our guiding Scripture, we focused on great issues of the day—poverty, racism, hunger, AIDS, illiteracy, justice, education, crime. We explored together what Christians must do to overcome the terrible problems and meet the needs of the least of us, and we heard the message repeated over and over that none of us can do it alone. We can't expect others to do for us what we must do for ourselves, and we are under a divine imperative to do what we can with what we have for those who cannot do for themselves.

At the closing session, Jimmy Carter shared from his own life with uncommon transparency and vulnerability. Nobel Peace prizewinner, human rights advocate, world leader and negotiator of peace, writer, carpenter, and Sunday school teacher, Mr. Carter described a crisis of faith in his early life that pushed him to take action. Later, some of us told each other how, as he was talking, we were remembering how this man who has become a statesman among us had been censured by the Southern Baptist Convention and thinking about how that must have hurt him to have his own group treat him as they did.

What other greatness is right here among us?

Who might we miss because he or she doesn't fit our profile?

What prophet is here whose message we don't want to hear, but must?

Whose gifts are still waiting to be discovered, developed, and expressed?

I was in some of the annual meetings of the Southern Baptist Convention when, upon hearing Mr. Carter's name from the podium, the crowd would go crazy, hissing and booing and jeering. When my husband

and I, in the crowd, did not participate, others would turn to us and say, "What are you—*liberals*?"

Those memories were long forgotten until Mr. Carter told us in Atlanta of learning an important lesson about faith and love from a man with whom he shared a missions project. Mr. Carter told that this man who taught him this lesson was not as well educated or affluent as he, but that he knew something vital and important about faith. As we listened, you could have heard a pin drop. I wept, and so did others.

"Love the Lord your God with all of your mind, heart, and soul," Mr. Carter's teacher told him, "and love the person standing in front of you as you would yourself."

Love God. Love one another. Love the person standing in front of you.

Has that been tried yet?

Back at home, I heard the criticisms of our meeting in Atlanta. I heard the skeptics and naysayers ridicule the event, its leaders, and those of us who attended and had experienced the power of the presence of God in our midst. Finally, I told a friend with as much compassion as I could muster, "I understand that we've been with all of the people you love to hate, but nothing you can say can take away from the power of that experience for me."

Always, and perhaps foremost in our intentional, new way of spirituality, we are called to a life of radical forgiveness, uncommon mercy, and unrelenting grace, and that is perhaps the hardest part of living in love together. *We are called to give that, however, because that is what we have been given!*

I don't get romantic feelings or become sentimental about the hard work of becoming conscious, being transformed, or living in relationship with other human beings. Life together is, in fact, so difficult and messy that I don't wonder at all that people often prefer the safe "church" of television evangelists, the substitute life of soap operas, and the heavily defended intimacy of Internet relationships!

Perhaps what we need is forgiveness if we are going to live with each other. All of us need it and all of us need to give it, and it may be the art and practice that we need to put at the top of our priorities in living together—teaching it, practicing it, and modeling it.

We all fail each other. We betray each other and are betrayed. We hurt each other, offend each other, and use each other for our own purposes.

Forgiveness isn't something we need now and then; forgiveness needs to flow through us constantly. It needs to be something we know how to do.

I've heard a story about a man who was a guest in a home, and when the family gathered for dinner on the first night, the head of the family made quite a pronouncement, welcoming the guest. "We want you to make yourself at home here," the host said. "In fact, we will just treat you as one of the family."

The guest turned white at the thought of being treated like one of the family, excused himself from the table, returned to his guest room, and packed his bags, leaving quietly by the side door. He was seen at the airport, leaving on a jet plane.

Indeed, it is within the sacred space of family—family of origin, family of faith—that the wrongs that are committed against each other hurt the most. It is from family members—the people we value most, the people who are supposed to be worthy of our trust, and the people with whom we are most vulnerable, the people we love and who love us—that our deepest wounds are felt, and so it is within family that the potential also exists for the deepest and most profound healing and forgiveness.

I've learned the hard way about forgiveness, giving it and receiving it, and what I have learned is that forgiveness is not only what you do, but, more than anything, *it is a way of being in the world.* It is laced with grace and mercy that flow from the understanding that we humans are flawed and finite. We are fallible creatures who cannot keep from hurting each other out of ignorance, carelessness, willfulness, and nearly always out of our own selfishness and self-centeredness.

Forgiveness as a way of being in the world is not about excusing the inexcusable. It is not about living in a rosy haze of denial or saccharine sweetness. It is about living in balance with two truths at the same time: We all could do better than we do, and most of us are doing the best we can. We don't do the best we know, and that is our growing edge.

Forgiveness is a choice to step into the redemptive rhythm of God at work in the world and change that which is harmful. It is a choice to own your part of the problem, to take conscious, intentional, and repetitive steps to stop repeating hurtful patterns and do the hard, laborious, and tedious work of establishing new patterns of grace that affirm the value and dignity of the life of each other.

There are two ways we can live—either out of fear or out of love—and it seems to me that God's way is the way of love. Love requires us to forgive and to be forgiven, and where we cannot yet do that, love requires that we be willing to be willing.

"Resentment," my friend Jerry Stephens says, "is like taking poison and waiting for the other person to die."

A startling statement about the negative force of resentment comes from Minako Ohba, Japanese short story writer: "By putting his hand around my neck, he slowly strangled himself." Indeed, the harm we inflict on others ultimately comes back to us. I cannot help connecting this quote with the idea of what the masculine energies, pushed too far, do to the feminine energies. Likewise, our feminine energies, pushed too far, devour us and suck the life from others.

Forgiveness is radical defiance in the face of that which would make you bitter. It is not a fist in the face of our hurts and our enemies, but an open hand that says, "I will forgive you," and another hand that says, "but I will not allow you to do that again."

On what had to have been the muggiest day of the year, Martus and I stood in line for almost three hours to get into the gym at Rice University in order to hear the Dalai Lama speak. For most of his speech, he was his usual happy and calm self, but when he responded to a question about forgiveness, his voice became strong and bold. "You are hurting another person when you allow him to abuse you. You must not let him do that, for it is a violation of both of you."

Forgiveness says, "I am willing to use my imagination to picture a new way for us to live together." It provides an opportunity to correct unhealthy dynamics, to reestablish boundaries instead of walls or to build them where there were none. It gives us an opportunity to renegotiate our relationships so that we move intentionally toward treating the people we say matter to us most as persons, created in the image of God, instead of as roles or objects who are there to serve us or please us.

Forgiveness is an invitation to step out onto the razor's edge of risk with the people with whom we have the most to lose and say, if we are the wrongdoer, "I was wrong. I am sorry. Will you forgive me?" and if we are the wronged, "I forgive you, but we must do things differently."

Forgiveness sometimes comes quickly, and sometimes it is about small things. Sometimes, forgiveness is a long process, and to rush it is to cheapen it. If you live long enough, you may experience a Big Hurt. We humans are infinitely creative in the ways we can betray and hurt each other, and if we forgive too soon, we dishonor the impact of what has been done.

Sometimes we forgive in increments as we work through the layers of the hurt, and sometimes it feels as if the hurt has no bottom. Sometimes one event can trigger a journey down into the deep, dark places where something has been festering for a long time, and that journey can be scary. Not taking it is scarier.

Forgiveness often is most powerful when we cannot give it, when the hurt is so deep that we are thrown back once again to the mat of failure and forced to admit our powerlessness over our own need to get revenge or get even.

A friend told me of being unable to pray the Lord's Prayer because she could not forgive someone who had hurt her deeply. Sometimes, being willing to be willing is the best you can do, but God can work even with that.

Forgiveness in the family is peacemaking at the most basic level of our society. If I were running the world, I would make learning how to own your own stuff, confess your part of the problem, make amends, and give and receive forgiveness part of school curricula. If it is not done in the schools, it must be done in the churches if we are going to have any impact or relevance in the world.

Forgiveness within the family and within the family of faith may be the hardest thing you will ever do. I suppose if it weren't hard, more people would be doing it, but forgiveness is a resounding yes to the healing, transforming, liberating, and empowering love of God, a yes to the divine and dynamic energy that longs to move freely and abundantly in us and among us, setting us free from the prisons of our own making, our petty grudges, and our deepest wounds.

There came a time in my life when I had worked and struggled to earn the forgiveness of a person who was important to me. Over a long period of time, I worked with my Twelve Steps sponsor to determine what was my part, and what was not. Finally, I had to come to terms with the fact that this person did not want to participate in forgiveness with me. "Respect her enough," my sponsor said, "to set her free not to love you, like you, or forgive you."

I have learned that forgiveness does its mighty work even in the midst of that which is incomplete and imperfect and through those of us who are fallible and finite.

A young man went to his priest and related a lifetime of abuse inflicted on him by relatives. "You must forgive them," the priest told him week after week, but the young man could not do it. The priest grew impatient with the young man, and the young man's despair grew weekly. Finally, one day, there was a shift.

"I was sitting in the chapel, praying that I could forgive them. I kept repeating the words you gave me about how they didn't know what they were doing, just like Jesus did on the cross," the young man said. He began to weep. "I looked up at that cross and thought about what it took for Jesus to say that. I have to tell you: those people did know what they were doing. They did it intentionally. They did it repeatedly. They laughed at me when they did it . . . and I forgive them, anyway."

I have learned that forgiveness is sometimes unbearably costly, but it's not nearly as costly as unforgiveness.

Grace is the yes of God, at work in the midst of our failures and our flaws. Grace is the loving provision of the Patient One who granted us the awesome gift and burden of free will. It is the mercy of the Compassionate One who knew that we would take the bounty of life and waste it, the gifts of creation and misuse them, and the opportunities of life and turn them into problems.

Grace is God's answer to our tendencies to choose darkness over light, curse over blessing, and death over life, and it is my belief that the hound of heaven who chases us up and down the pathways of our lives is all about grace, and God will not let us go until we learn that lesson.

Forgiveness has the power to unite that which has been separated, to bring together that which has been torn asunder, and to connect the forces of good in each of us for the benefit of the larger world.

Standing on the sidewalk between the shell of the old cathedral in Coventry, England, and the new, modern one, I gaze at the cross that unites the two buildings. I'd just walked slowly, reverently around the old cathedral, a witness to the horrors of World War II and the unimaginable hatred that could make someone bomb a house of worship and, as well, to the power of forgiveness and the work of reconciliation.

Weeping, I walked slowly between the two buildings, remembering my bedrock belief that God is at work in all things, attempting to bring about good. This dramatic setting reminded me then and continues to come to me to restore my faith in the One who is working to reconcile us first to himself and then to each other.

Joining forces with each other, we are united by the powerful force of love, and as we join forces, we must commit to be intentional, focused, and deliberate (all masculine strengths) as we are patient, receptive, and nourishing (feminine strengths) to each other.

We are being called to a new way of loving each other; we must learn how to love with agape love, the love that *lets be.*

We are being called from confusion to understanding. We are being asked to give up blame and take on the art and skill of empathy. We are being invited to compete on the appropriate playing fields, but also learn how to cooperate and collaborate for the good of each other. It is possible for us to move from the neurotic imbalance of patriarchy to a balance that includes both feminine and masculine strengths.

We are being called from power moves and power struggles to acts of love, and the movement of love begins with the individual and within the individual, moving out in ripples of healing love to a world in desperate need.

Each of us must live in two worlds, in the world of our own separateness and individuality and in the larger world of community. Joining forces within and joining forces without are tasks worthy of a life.

Questions for Reflection and Discussion

1. What have you learned about yourself from reading this book? What has made you uncomfortable? What has given you hope?

2. What have you decided to do as a result of reading this book? Where are you encouraged to take responsibility for your own life in new ways?

3. If you buy into the idea of forgiveness as a lifestyle, what would that mean for your life? How could it change your life?

4. What is the difference between authentic forgiveness and living in denial? between forgiveness and looking the other way, pretending something doesn't hurt, excusing something as an act of "peace at any price"?

5. What person do you need to forgive most?

Taking Action

1. Read Jesus' mission statement in Luke 4:18-19. Decide if this is an initiative in which you'd like to participate. How will you do that?

2. Let forgiveness into your life. If you need a 12 Step sponsor, a confessor, a priest, pastor or spiritual director, an analyst, or a therapist to guide you through this process, find one.

4. Join forces with fellow seekers and pilgrims. Participate intentionally in a community of love and faith, as imperfect and flawed as it may be.

5. Love God. Love yourself. Love others. Love generously. Love again.